Post-Traumatic Faith

"*Post-Traumatic Faith* is the prescription faith leaders give others, but we forget to take ourselves. E. Jill Riley's authenticity and candor invite us to see ourselves through the looking glass of her journey and engage in the uncomfortable, yet necessary, lifelong task of healing."

—**William Mack III**, pastoral counselor and spiritual director

"*Post-Traumatic Faith* is a courageous and unflinching account of E. Jill Riley's efforts to recover from a childhood that was horrifically abusive. Riley takes an honest look at what happened to her, how the abuse impacted her ability to function in the real world, and finally how one cannot escape one's past until they take the time to confront it directly. Riley's recovery is an inspiration, and her ability to retain any semblance of faith after what she went through is a testament to her own willingness to transform pain into power."

—**Russell Rowland**, author of *Fifty-Six Counties: A Montana Journey*

"E. Jill Riley invites us to explore what it's like to grow up in traumatic environments, strive for success in every area of life, receive diagnoses of complex-PTSD and DID, and still choose to love God and the people in her life. Her writing is compelling, honest, and heart-wrenching—and it is also filled with grace, kindness, and hope. I couldn't put the book down."

—**Alaine Buchanan**, dean, College of Graduate and Professional Studies, North Central University

"I applaud E. Jill Riley for her courage to tell her story. I pray it will open doors for conversation with others who have suffered abuse in hopes that it can lead to their healing and wholeness. I have worked with trauma victims for decades and this book offers hope."

—**Mark Novak**, former executive minister of the ordered ministry, Evangelical Covenant Church

"A well-written story about complex issues told with dignity and humor. It asks timely questions about faith, mental illness, and the current Christian culture. I hope it gets you to consider your attitude about mental illness and faith."

—**Nancy McGrade**, licensed clinical professional counselor

Post-Traumatic Faith

E. Jill Riley

Foreword by James H. Peak

CASCADE Books • Eugene, Oregon

POST-TRAUMATIC FAITH

Copyright © 2024 E. Jill Riley. All rights reserved. Except for brief quotations in critical publications or reviews, no part of this book may be reproduced in any manner without prior written permission from the publisher. Write: Permissions, Wipf and Stock Publishers, 199 W. 8th Ave., Suite 3, Eugene, OR 97401.

Cascade Books
An Imprint of Wipf and Stock Publishers
199 W. 8th Ave., Suite 3
Eugene, OR 97401

www.wipfandstock.com

PAPERBACK ISBN: 978-1-6667-7788-8
HARDCOVER ISBN: 978-1-6667-7789-5
EBOOK ISBN: 978-1-6667-7790-1

Cataloguing-in-Publication data:

Names: Riley, E. Jill, author. | Peak, James H., foreword.

Title: Post-traumatic faith / E. Jill Riley ; foreword by James H. Peak.

Description: Eugene, OR : Cascade Books, 2024

Identifiers: ISBN 978-1-6667-7788-8 (paperback) | ISBN 978-1-6667-7789-5 (hardcover) | ISBN 978-1-6667-7790-1 (ebook)

Subjects: LCSH: Riley, E. Jill. | Post-traumatic stress disorder—21st century—Social aspects—United States. | Post-traumatic stress disorder—Patients—Biography. | Post-traumatic stress disorder—Patients. | Mind and body.

Classification: BR1725.R578 A3 2024 (paperback) | BR1725.R578 A3 (ebook)

VERSION NUMBER 08/23/24

Contents

Foreword by James H. Peak | vii
Introduction | xi

1 The Super Moon | 1
2 Human Pin Cushion | 6
3 Operation Perfection | 10
4 Loaner Parents | 15
5 The Yellow Rope | 19
6 Oldest | 23
7 Beautiful Ball of Nothing | 26
8 Middle | 31
9 Living in Church | 38
10 Sandy | 43
11 Shared Space | 47
12 Meeting the Aryan Nations | 52
13 Basement Candy | 56
14 Canned Promises | 59
15 Dirty Laundry | 63
16 Moving On | 68

Contents

17 Hallmark Holiday | 71
18 Technicolor | 78
19 When Churches Are Assholes | 82
20 Girls Can Too! | 89
21 Mosquitos and Lord Ladimore | 93
22 I'm Batman | 96
23 Pac-Man Sucks | 99
24 Suicide Surges | 102
25 Multiplied Me | 106
26 Christmas Cactus | 111
27 Zoot, Emeraude, and Molly | 118
28 God of My Understanding | 122
29 Grave Robbing | 126
30 Window Shopping | 129
31 Surviving Childhood | 132

Afterword | 140

Foreword

Dr. Peak was my psychiatrist for three years. He was of tremendous help to me during some of the toughest recovery years.

Your brain is not designed to make you happy. It is designed to keep you alive.

No one knows this truth better than the patient who copes with complex-PTSD (C-PTSD) as the result of childhood trauma and neglect.

Many of us are familiar with the diagnosis of post-traumatic stress disorder (PTSD) from learning about the combat experiences of war veterans. A GI in Iraq, blessed with a normal childhood and upbringing, is on patrol when his squad leader accidentally triggers a hidden IED. The soldier is knocked down by the deafening concussive shock. His brain reactively etches each sensation into long-term emotional memory, including details such as the time of day, the shape of the sunglasses that melted on his buddy's face, the quality of light in the adjacent courtyard, the white dog with a brown side marking that ducked into the alley just before the explosion.

Months after the accident, he might still re-experience the trauma in nightmares when he sees that white dog with a brown side marking and run desperately away, waiting for the fatal concussive thump only to spring awake drenched in sweat. He might find himself unaccountably frightened of places back home where he cannot see behind corners or down alleyways. And when the light shines at a certain time of the day he finds himself vigilant, angry, and overwhelmed. He is experiencing symptoms of dissociation. His body is back home in Montana, but his brain is still on patrol in Fallujah.

Complex-PTSD, a condition we are just starting to understand, is different. It generally develops in people exposed to trauma and neglect multiple times, usually during childhood. It is what happens to the baby living with their alcoholic or addicted mother. It is the little boy who has been told yet again, "Just wait until your father gets home," shaking, while lying in bed—waiting. It is the child that hears yet another foster parent sadly telling the state worker, "We just can't handle him. He hides food in his bedroom and pees in the closet. He is just too disturbed to stay here."

These are children who grew up in families where the caretaking and parenting was ineffective, inconsistent, or both.

What do you do when you are small, alone, and scared? Maybe you focus on something in the room, a blanket, or a toy, and hyper-focus on it, so you do not have to focus on what an adult is doing to you, something you have no ability to control? Or you might imagine you are somewhere else, or someone else.

How confusing it must be that the person who is supposed to love and protect you is the one who hurts you. Even more perplexing is when that same person is loving one day, angry the next, pleasantly sober in the morning, but terrifyingly out of control at night.

The core symptoms of PTSD include re-experiencing the trauma while awake ("flashbacks") or in nightmares, avoidance of any thoughts or sensations associated with the event ("triggers"), negative thinking about oneself and the world, and generalized hyper arousal or hyper vigilance.

In addition to the above, the complex-PTSD patient often has impairments in these other areas, emotional regulation, relationships, and identity/sense of self.

Chronically traumatized individuals live in contradiction. Their brain trains them to stay emotionally numb under mundane circumstances in a desperate attempt to avoid the fight or flight response triggered by emotional reactions and traumatic memories. Even their friends and partners can experience them as cold, aloof, or emotionally distant. But when the numbing no longer works, and the C-PTSD sufferer believes they are returning to a dangerous situation the sufferer can become quickly agitated, inconsolable, or even violent.

This lack of emotional regulation frequently results in intense, chaotic, and unstable relationships, particularly with romantic partners. The abandoned, neglected child within alternates between a desperate neediness for love with an uncontrollable fear of and rage toward rejection, triggered by thoughts and memories long buried and only half-understood.

Finally, even the sense of self can be impaired. Memories can be so painful that the brain actively avoids thinking about them. The frightened child who learns to live in an imaginary world because the real one is so frightening starts living there even when things are safe. These kids are learning dissociation, how to have your brain and body disconnected. They are physically there, but it feels like you are talking with someone else, and when you ask a dissociative person about a recent conversation, do not be surprised when they honestly cannot remember anything about it. The most extreme and sensationalized example of this phenomena is dissociative identity disorder (DID, popularly called "multiple personality disorder"). My years as a psychiatrist suggest to me that DID is very rare, but milder forms of clinically significant dissociation are quite common, but almost never recognized.

As you read *Post-Traumatic Faith* you will experience a moving, genuine account of what it feels like to live with C-PTSD. The memory gaps, that sense of being an imposter despite performing with breathtaking competence, the desperate attempt to keep moving ever forward, believing that to stop is oblivion.

And finally, the blessed, painful, inevitable unraveling of it all.

It is heartbreaking that so many children are raised in abusive or ineffective homes. These kids have high ACE (Adverse Childhood Experience) scores which correlate with higher rates of both mental and physical disabilities as adults.

But here is the light, the miracle, buried deep in what seems at first to be impenetrable darkness.

Somehow, someway, there are people born with such strength, courage and grace that they conquer these seemingly insurmountable obstacles and lead lives of great positive purpose and meaning. I know this to be true. You are holding the evidence in your hand.

Jill suffers from severe C-PTSD. But that does not alter the fact that she is smart, dedicated, and capable of seeing beauty and humor in even the

Foreword

most difficult of situations. God loves Jill. She knows it. That will get you through a lot. Anything, actually.

Jill is a successful pastor, author, and speaker. She has raised wonderful children. Hers is a heart of forgiveness and love. A beautiful rose growing in inhospitable climates.

Of course, it came at a price. We can only wall off the painful realities of the past for so long. Running from demons is human. Facing them is the practical expression of spiritual belief. When we do so, things fall apart, and they did for Jill.

Lying in the ruins of the life we imagined we were living is excruciatingly painful and disorientating. But if we are brave, realize we are never alone, and reach out to others along the way, we can piece together the shards of our shattered innocence, reclaim our memories, and even forgive the unforgiveable.

When we do this we embrace the hurting child that lies deep inside and model to all humanity the grace and dignity of an authentic life in God.

James H. Peak MD
Billings, Montana

Introduction

"People will want to know that there is hope," a friend said after I mentioned writing a book about my life. "They will want to find something to encourage them." "Yes!" I thought. "Don't we all!" While my story, on the surface, may not inspire hope, if you look deeper there is a bedrock of faith in it. The potential of hope gives me traction on days when my emotions are slick tires on ice, pulls me out of the quicksand of depression, and displays a lighthouse when I think I'm lost and drowning.

These days I consider my faith with some affection and a lot of desperation. I cling to it like a life raft, tentatively hopeful in its ability to actually buoy me. The bright, shiny, helium-filled faith of my youth has been replaced with one of deep abiding conviction and unrequited questions.

Throughout my life I have found God in unexpected places, tucked in pockets, peeking out just enough so I knew he was there. My inner strength was formed during quiet little intrigues and dark night hours talking with God. He quietly handed me the strength to dry my tears, with reassurance that he was always there.

This is the holy quest is it not? To find God even when life is at its most challenging? I share my stories with the hope of awakening our blurred senses to the moments where God tiptoed into our hearts speaking reassurance, comfort, and peace.

Introduction

The singular factor that has given me strength and courage is my faith. All that I am is upheld by that. Faith is something bigger than myself, gives me purpose, and fills me with understanding that I exist for more than myself.

"Shame is carried guilt," the therapist said. I had not really given the concept of shame much thought. Whose guilt am I carrying? Is this why I have never felt good enough? Smart enough? Beautiful enough? I have always felt inadequate, no matter the category of accomplishment. There was always someone more talented, better-looking, or smarter. Perhaps this is why I have never felt "worthy" of love. I have always felt like I had to earn love, but it was a carrot before a horse—I could never quite get there.

I consistently strive to be perfect—an unobtainable goal. The therapist said, "Perfectionism is a self-destructive and addictive belief system. We experience shame and judgement because of perfectionism." Well color me purple! I didn't know that. I just thought I had to be the best, no matter the cost. The truth is I am terrified of being wrong, last, or least.

My identity has always been inextricably linked to what others thought. External appearances were the only things that mattered. So it's no wonder that I became addicted to that saccharine song of approval.

The fact is, life offers all of us circumstances that challenge our spirit and resiliency. Survival is a personal journey for which I have few answers and many questions. Our challenges come in varying degrees of difficulty, such that we cannot compare those to one another. What causes one person to survive feels like a roll of the dice, a luck of the draw. But there is hope on every page. I know that because I'm still alive and able to write my story.

God is good. All the time.

1

The Super Moon

ON THE NIGHT OF the super moon in 2015, I sat watching the lunar phenomenon, my skin sticky from the Arizona heat. Backlit by the eclipsing moon, little hills gave form to the otherwise unshapely landscape, rising and falling in shallow breaths out of the desert. I paid homage to the majestic mountains of my home state, Montana, by mocking the desert hills who thought themselves big. I narrowed my eyes and tipped my head to the right just a little so the blood-red moon bloomed from the top of the lumpy old palm tree in front of me. If it weren't for the fact that I was in a psychiatric hospital, the scene would have been magical.

If someone had told me two weeks prior to the blood moon that I would become a patient in a psych facility, I would have called them crazy. I was the pastor of a growing church, in the process of launching a community center. I had more speaking engagements than I could keep up with and was writing for two magazines. My side job as a corporate consultant and executive trainer was going well, and I had started a photography business. Our three teenagers at home were maturing right on schedule, and our adult child was serving in the armed forces. In the arduous land of adulthood, I was killing it.

I was pastoring a church I loved where I fought to establish a culturally sensitive, open-minded community. It was an amazing community but tragedy upon tragedy seemed to besiege our congregation at every turn.

Post-Traumatic Faith

Laura was a beautiful, fun-loving lady. She had blond ringlets, bright blue eyes, and her sunny disposition made her delightful to be around. I loved having her as a part of our congregation.

On a December Sunday in 2013, after I finished preaching at the Mexican restaurant where we met for church, she gave me a friendly wave as she scootched out of the restaurant booth she was sitting in and headed out the door. I regretted not being able to talk to her following our church gathering.

On the previous Friday, she had cleared off her computer at the party store where she served as a planner and cleaned out her desk. On that Monday she addressed letters to her family and loved ones, telling each how much they meant to her. She signed her will and testament and a living will/do not resuscitate order. Laura started dinner for her mom and dad and left the house around 4:45 p.m. She drove to a wooded area, put her favorite country song on repeat on her iPod, stepped out of her car, and shot herself in the chest.

When I arrived at her house shortly after her suicide, we looked over the box of letters and papers she had left. Her severe depression had seemed to have loosed its grasp on her of late. But everything was so meticulous and organized, it was clear that she had planned to kill herself for quite some time. She seemed stable and happy. Nobody suspected she had reached the end of her hope.

The next day Laura's parents and I went to the funeral home to view her body. The mortician pulled me aside and said, "There is something I need to tell you before the family goes in. She is smiling. It's important the family know that we cannot manipulate the body postmortem to create a smile. She was smiling when she died." Thirty-three years old and Laura was happy to be dead.

I worked with the family through the tragedy and on to the memorial service. The funeral chapel was filled with people, none of whom could understand her choice to die at thirty-three years of age, least of all me.

Laura's death left an indelible mark on me. In public, I soldiered on, carrying the family and friends through moments of grief, pain, and bewilderment. I smiled in the company of others and cried in private.

The Super Moon

In another moment of trauma, I was thrust into an awkward and painful situation. The African American, Puerto Rican, and Native American students of our congregation had a dance crew. They practiced in a repurposed room loaned to them from the local men's shelter. Sometimes I would go and sit with them, enduring the loud pumping music, just to watch them dance and to show my support. One night the mama of the group called and asked me to come down to the studio.

A couple from Chicago had come to town, having family roots here. The two of them ran a prostitution ring and also acted as drug carrying "mules." (Billings is on a major North/South and East/West highway corridor, so trafficking of all kinds is prevalent here.) Two men identifying themselves as FBI officers broke into their shabby little hotel room and kidnapped them both. The girl was released safely. Unbeknownst to her, her partner, her pimp, was taken out and shot execution style, one bullet in the back of his head. I met the girl at the dance studio. She was concerned about her boyfriend's whereabouts and well-being. The ministry of presence was all I could offer during this confusing time. Not long after I arrived, we received the call that he had been executed. I held this young woman while she screamed for the man she depended on and loved. Another tragedy. Another death to absorb.

A small Puerto Rican man had joined our congregation. He was a recently released felon who needed help and relationship to establish himself in the community. I met him through the local men's shelter. Jorge became a regular part of our church congregation. He was always there to help out if I needed him to. One day he was agitated, restless, and paranoid. The Veteran Affairs hadn't filled his PTSD meds and wouldn't be able to for several days. My office was on the third floor, above a Mexican restaurant, and as I wandered down to the first-floor restaurant on a break from work, I saw Jorge. He asked me to join him for dinner—he was struggling and obviously needed some attention, so I joined him.

As we sat eating dinner, the owner's mentally unstable nephew began to circle us, taunting Jorge and baiting him to a fight. As the situation escalated, both men grabbed sharp steak knives and began to threaten each other. Being the only person in that section of the restaurant, I summoned up some unusual strength, wedged myself between them, and physically pushed the nephew through the restaurant away from us, placing him under the watchful eye of the uncle. Once safely in my office Jorge pulled an eight-inch knife with a gut hook on the end out of his pocket and gave it to me, afraid he would do something with it that he would regret. It terrified me to know how close I had come to harm since I was positioned in between the two men and their knives.

In that same year, 2015, we moved my office into buildings owned by the local shelter. The walls were thin and the building cavernous. Residents and employees of the shelter wandered in and out with some regularity, leaving me with little privacy or security. Our building was the last one on the city block before the shelter. Men who couldn't get into the shelter, either because they were sexual offenders or not sober, would gather underneath our building's portico, drinking, smoking, and talking the hours away. My office shared a wall with the front doors. I would sit in the office and hear the men talk about me with sexual innuendos.

I bought a gun. I took a gun safety course and got my concealed carry license so I would feel like I had some protection if any of the men confronted me during the late hours I kept at the office.

The fear and burden of living life around potentially harmful individuals and those who lived on the margin became palpable. My nervous system was consistently jacked up waiting for the next emergency. The stress, lack of sleep, and emotions were pummeling me. My workaholic self just kept plugging along, feeling as if I were carrying the weight of the world. The busyness of raising four children, a stress-filled marriage while maintaining four jobs kept me running on adrenaline, which softened the interior walls of my mental health until it disintegrated under the strain.

Friends, family, and peers chastised me with their words, while also stroking my ego and patting me on the back. I produced for others, and they liked it. I liked it, even though I worked until my chest hurt so bad I would curl up on my office floor until the burn subsided. I was late to everything and rushed through every conversation and event like a racehorse with blinders on. My frenzy kept the emotional pain of a tragic childhood hidden from me. If I was busy, I didn't have time to consider myself.

I was lulled into the crucible of being in demand—being needed. However, being needed is not a purpose or life goal in itself. It can become a toxin that hardens the soul from the outside in, like a loaf of bread left on the counter for days. What once was soft, nurturing, and absorbent becomes hard, inviting mold and corruption. Our souls need to be kept soft to absorb light, nutrients, and warmth. It's not that being in a caretaking roll will kill your soul. It is prioritizing others, to the neglect of your soul, that corrupts. My mind knew this, but my heart did not.

By summer 2015, my bosses—a director in charge of helping me start the church and a national office liaison to churches—decided I should attend a workshop on childhood trauma. I was exhausted. My internal mental and emotional scaffolding was a twisted wreck. Feelings of displacement, hollowness, deep depression, and anxiety had taken over my life. My boss thought it would be good for me to explore how my traumatic childhood had affected my life.

The decision was made that I would step away from the church for a time to work on our marriage and on my mental health. I was devastated.

Despite the accumulating stress and my crumbling world, I told the director and church liaison that I wasn't about to attend the conference on trauma. At one time my sister had engaged in trauma treatment, and it led to her addiction and death. I had no wish to go down that road. They signed me up and bought me a plane ticket anyway. Bastards.

2

Human Pin Cushion

When I arrived for the conference in Arizona in September 2015, my bad attitude swelled with the heat. I caught the clinic's van from the airport to an old stucco hotel, a retired Best Western where I would be spending my time at night after the clinic released us for the day. The bedraggled hotel had ceased to be "best" some time ago and had clearly settled on just being a dusty, western establishment.

The morning of the workshop arrived, and I treated myself to some rubbery eggs and nasty coffee in the hotel lobby. There were a few other people eating, so I assumed, correctly, they were going to the workshop too. One of the men looked disheveled, practically hung over. The others seemed as flatly enthused as I felt. We rode to the clinic in silence.

Upon arrival, my van mates and I joined thirty or so others in a large room. Half of the people were patients from the attached psychiatric addiction and trauma hospital. They were loud, raucous, and opinionated. My initial reaction to being surrounded by patients was that I was afraid they were carriers of some mental diseases that I didn't want to catch.

The director began our session with, "You have now embarked on a three-to-five-year journey of trauma healing." In my head I responded, "Listen, sister. I signed up for three to five days. That is all you're getting." My personal investment in this process could not have been less. Also, in my mind I was barely there for information, certainly not participation.

As the director began to explain what our experience would be during the week, I became more and more nervous. We would be divided into small groups. We were going to delve into our past and share our personal histories. Out loud. It had all the elements of bad news.

When the therapists introduced themselves, I sat sizing them up. There was the young professional who was leading. She seemed compassionate and grown up. I approved. There were a couple of therapists who looked as if they were not yet out of high school, certainly not yet out of college. I did not approve. There were two practitioners who had some air of gravitas and professionalism that I could appreciate. And then there was a frumpy older therapist, Anita, who seemed like somebody's grandmother. In Anita's introduction she spoke of being an alcoholic in recovery, and I liked her immediately; she knew who she was and was open enough to share that with a room of strangers. Luck of the draw. She became my therapist.

One therapist to five or six participants and damned if the patients weren't intermingled with the workshop participants. The therapy sessions included teaching about emotions, abuse, relationships, self-esteem, and childhood trauma. It was deep, clinical, personal—and terrifying. My own traumatic past started to eke its way out from the shadows and into a brighter focus. I began to understand why I needed to be there.

We sat against the wall in a straight row of chairs, facing our therapist, Anita. Even though it was summer in the desert, we were wrapped in blankets. This wasn't a therapeutic tool. It was survival. The room was frigid due to overactive air conditioning. We sat in a dimly lit room, cocooned in grey, scratchy blankets, listening to one another's stories of love, loss, abuse, and heartache. As the other women shared, I was terrified for my turn.

On the third day of the workshop, it was my turn in the "hot seat." In the darkened room, I sat in the center, with the therapist sitting to my right, just out of my peripheral vision. The group members gave silent witness to our conversation. The therapist began asking questions about my past, based on a preliminary questionnaire I had filled out days before.

In 1980, in Coeur d'Alene, Idaho, as an eight-year-old child, I ran away from home because I was terrified of my mother, Marilyn. I knew she was going to beat me, and I had to get away. The infraction? I folded some dirty clothes and put them in my drawer instead of in the hamper. Why? I don't know. I just remember it made sense to my eight-year-old brain. As Marilyn began to rant, I ran out of the house, my fear that I would be caught pushing me on. She caught up with me three blocks later. She was an imposing 5'10" angry Irish woman with sharp green eyes that seemed to get brighter the angrier she got. I was a petite Korean girl. She grabbed and pulled me, feet dragging on the sidewalk, around the block back toward our house with a big 2 x 4 board in her hand. We walked past a couple out for a mid-day walk. I begged them with my eyes to save me. Marilyn transformed herself into a bright and pleasant conversationalist, all the while holding me with a death grip. After some small talk, the walkers waved brightly and walked on.

She dragged me into the basement, backing me up against the plain cement wall. I looked behind the old wood stove to see if I could hide there but the fireplace was lit so it was too hot. I studied the open hole in the concrete, to the crawl space under the porch and wondered whether I could hide there, but that big dark hole was also frightening. She grabbed me and began beating me across the back, the front—anything she could reach. At one point, as I writhed on the floor to get away from her, she grabbed me by the feet and pulled off my shoes. She began beating my feet over and over until they were on fire. I curled up in a ball on the floor, receiving blow after blow, praying for her to stop. Obviously, her rage was exceedingly disproportionate to my transgression.

As Anita asked me questions about the incident, I was confused as she interrupted me with meaningless bits of information. I heard her telling me the names of the women in the group, as if I didn't know they were there. She pointed out different shapes, colors, and objects displayed around the room.

I didn't know that I was in the midst of a dissociative episode. As I told the story, I mentally and emotionally fell into it. Past became present. I was suddenly that small child backed up against the rough, gray, cement wall, peering around the wood-burning stove to see if I could hide there, away from Marilyn's screaming and her huge board. My peers later told me I looked and sounded as if I were the childhood version of myself receiving a beating. The little bits of information Anita fed me were intended to orient me back to the room and current reality. I had just mentally disappeared into myself.

For the rest of the day's sessions, throughout the meals and into the evening, I was sweating and disoriented, disturbed by what had happened. Sleep that night was in short supply, interrupted by nightmares, shaking, and cold sweats.

The next day, still somewhat confused and now exhausted, I returned to the workshop. During our morning break, Anita said to me, "the director would like to talk with you." I knocked on the director's office door. The director was warm and inviting, but I was significantly startled by the twenty long acupuncture needles stuck in her face and ears. I'm not sure what purpose they were serving. Maybe she was relieving tension. Most people settle for chocolate, Netflix, and a glass of wine.

We embarked on a very serious conversation about my mental health, based on some "regressions" they had seen. My regressions? I wasn't the one with needles sticking out of my face! At one point she picked up the phone to answer it and forgot momentarily to take the needles out of her ear before she put the receiver to her head. Oh, the irony. She was about to make her brain into a pin cushion, and I was the one who needed help?

I remember thinking, "someday I'm going to write about this." Hilarious though it was, my scrambled and traumatized brain did not register the gravitas of the moment. The end result was that she and my bosses talked me into becoming a patient at the hospital. I agreed to it because the clinicians and the church leadership said it was the right decision. But in the moment, I will have to say, I just felt lost and incapable of making that decision for myself.

Past this point, I was no longer left on my own. The white eighteen-passenger van and driver were summoned to take me to gather my things. The driver waited while I packed, returned emails, sent half-finished articles to editors, made arrangements for the family, shaved my legs, and checked out of the hotel. I was given approximately thirty minutes to do all that, with instructions that I leave the hotel room door open as I wrapped up my tasks.

We drove the short distance back to campus, to a section I was not familiar with. It was a guarded compound—not with razor wire or guards with assault rifles but by security guards with flashlights and pickup trucks. Even so, I felt like a captive. A quarter-square-mile campus of classrooms, therapy rooms, clinicians' offices, the cafeteria, and dorms was my cell.

Staff greeted me warmly and took my luggage. They explained they would be going through my bags. This was the first in a long series of intrusions on my privacy and independence. They took my phone, computer, shoelaces, the string from my running shorts, leg razor, privacy, and dignity. A tall, blond, pretty girl wandered by as they were sorting through my luggage. She saw my distressed and sad face and said to me, "Don't worry. It'll get better." Her reassurance comforted me. A little.

3

Operation Perfection

I KNEW THE TREATMENT facility cost $65,000. The patients in my small group had let that cat out of the bag. I don't know that I expected any sort of posh accommodations, but for all the world, this was not a luxurious setting. Walking into the buildings was a two-decade step back in time. Wood paneling, white linoleum floors, and a plain medical aesthetic greeted me. For two hours I sat in a bright room with heavy, carved wooden chairs and a single computer unit. An inpatient clerk came in and began asking questions, from simple to more complex, including whether I had any superpowers, heard voices, or was hallucinating that there were other people in the room.

I was assigned a pager circa 1982 so I could be summoned for appointments and medications. I learned that I was on "checks." This meant every hour or two somebody had to lay eyes on me to make sure I was okay.

Following dinner alone in the "intake room," which I couldn't stomach, they showed me to my room. My double room, reminiscent of an eighties dorm room, had a wardrobe, bed, shelf, and desk for each resident. A shared bathroom and plain double vanity completed the austere accommodations. The only item that bespoke luxury was the bathrobe folded neatly on the bed.

That was Thursday.

Newly admitted patients were segregated in rooms near the nurse's station, until medically cleared as safe and sober. The patients nicknamed this part of housing "the nursery." The nursery was a wide nurse's station surrounded by dorm rooms, medical offices, and the pharmacy. My room was the first room, two steps from the pharmacy, two steps to the nurse's station, and five steps from the front door. I was right in the middle of all the "action." Outside my door people picked up their mail and packages, asked for fifteen-minute "passes" to use their leg and face razors, or requested a squirt of cologne/perfume from one of the contraband glass bottles.

The staff dispensed medications three times a day so a line would form right outside my door morning, noon, and night. They interviewed new patients in a room four steps from my door so every new person passed my room. Late into the night the front door would bang, and there were loud conversations between nurses and patients. It was a chaotic setting to try and rest. Only sheer emotional exhaustion lulled me to sleep each night.

By Sunday I'd had enough. After three days of not doing anything except panicking, trembling, and crying, I was certain I had made a mistake. Three hours at a time in the fetal position while waves of panic and fear washed over me was too much.

And I was angry. Angry that I had to learn to breathe, think, and live through this nightmare. I told the staff I was leaving. Money be damned, I was not going to stay here. The lack of schedule, no interaction with other patients, or any formal productive activity had me convinced this was an exercise in futility and boredom. The staff arranged for me to talk to the resident psychiatric physician's assistant. She was big, jolly, and warm. I hastily explained that I was leaving. Her compassionate response? "You are *not* leaving." And then in a low, rushed voice, "I mean, you're really free to go, we can't keep you here." Then she jokingly added, "But you'll have to get through me first," referring to her large body versus my more petite one. "Look at me. Look at you. Look at me. Look at you." She made me laugh hard and encouraged me to hang on. Tomorrow would be better. There would be interaction, a schedule, and meaningful programming. Something in her demeanor reversed my decision, and I resigned myself to being cooperative.

This total loss of control can be alarming to grown-ups. Being told when to sleep, eat, recreate, and meditate can be demoralizing. But to be in a place where your every need is met, physically and emotionally, to be kept safe from all those who have hurt you, to be free to express anger or pain openly, without shame, is a luxury. There wasn't a day that went by that I didn't hate it. And yet every day since I have wished I could go back.

My therapist said it's because it is probably the first time I have ever felt completely safe and cared for. She's right.

A battery of computer assessments was the first step in diagnostic intervention. The assessment center was a small cave-like room, with a rounded-top hobbit door and buzzing, fluorescent lighting inside. Patients sat quietly in little computer cubicles answering question after question on their computers. The questions covered every kind of abuse, neglect, addiction, sexual compulsion, deviance, and perversion you can imagine. More than you can imagine. I felt so dirty after reading all those questions, partially because it put a spotlight on my own past, for which I felt shame and guilt, but also because I read things in those questions that my sheltered brain had never been exposed to. I did not want to know about people's sexual preferences and fantasies. I had no idea the lengths and depths people would go to hide their addiction. The questions on abuse were especially sad and familiar. The more questions I answered, the more I realized I was on the heavy end of the scale when it came to the severity of abuse. Later, in conversation with other patients, we expressed how weird and violating the tests were, while deep down knowing they achieved their purpose of pointing to the pain.

The psychiatrist, therapists, and medical doctors interviewed and evaluated me. They fired question after question at me about my past, each hitting wounds that had been festering. It was like Chinese water torture, a constant drip in the same spot in my mind that said, "You're hurting. You're sick. Your mother was a sociopath. Your family was f'in nuts."

Several days after the requisite testing, I met another psychiatrist. His office was bleak, old, with wood paneling, a simple desk shoved against the wall and dusty mini blinds doing their dead level best to keep out the Arizona heat. I sat on a 1970s-style vinyl green chair next to the desk. As we talked, he carefully and skillfully peeled back layers of denial and disbelief to expose my mental illness that had run unchecked for far too long. To see my life defined so thoroughly by a stranger, as deduced by computer tests, was fascinating and unsettling. It was as if he was reading my very mind. He carefully explained what each diagnosis meant. I was diagnosed with complex-PTSD (C-PSTD), a major depressive disorder, anxiety disorder, and dissociative identity disorder (DID). I was also diagnosed with dysthymia, another type of depression. The names of the illnesses were as overwhelming as the knowledge that they were incurable. I could learn to manage them, but they were hardwired into my body.

Operation Perfection

I thought depression was scalable from mild to severe. I never imagined there were variants! Together, major depressive disorder (MDD) and dysthymia make persistent depressive disorder (PDD), which means I got a double scoop—"double depression." Adding insult to injury, I was recently told that my depression is endogenous, meaning it has some internal causes or origin. Translation? My circumstances aren't entirely responsible for my depression; my chemical makeup is actually unbalanced. Depression isn't just going to "go away."

I also discovered that my feelings of everything being unmanageable and overwhelming were due to an anxiety disorder. Anxiety is worrying about a future that hasn't arrived and overconfidently predicting what might happen. I had been making emotional decisions about mirages.

One of my childhood games was Operation. I loved the challenge of trying to pull the bones out of the guy without making the obnoxious buzzer go off. I am confident Milton Bradley is at least partially responsible for my anxiety disorder. Between Operation and Perfection, I was set up for it. But before proper medication and therapy I felt like a walking Operation game. If somebody hit the wrong nerve, I felt like I would go through the roof.

Because they are illnesses with management strategies, not cures, I have imagined I was going to feel anxious and depressed for the rest of my life. On bad days, my emotions still tell me I am a deadweight, useless to society forever and always.

As intimidating as the entry process was, once I settled into the routines in the psych hospital, it became a cocoon. I felt safe. By the time I reached one week in residence, I didn't feel like the new kid anymore. They provided food, lodging, and medications. My general well-being was monitored, as was my mood and general disposition. There was no safer place to discover and explore my newly minted mental-illness diagnoses. Therapists doted on me, and psychiatrists carefully managed my treatment. The hospital experience was an odd mixture of acceptance and challenge for growth. All the residents had baggage and "stuff" and willingly seemed to accept that fact for themselves and for one another. We were all hurting and in need.

It felt honest. If somebody was having a rotten day, not only was it permissible to let it show (anger, tears, sullen faces, etc.), it was also okay to not have to fix everybody else's bad day. No platitudes or placating, just a simple "sorry you're having a bad day," or "sorry life is hard right now," or even better, a nod and walk away. In my forty-three years I had never been in an environment so accepting and dizzyingly communal.

One day I stood in the cafeteria and watched as a mom, also in treatment, tried to hug and reconcile with her two teen daughters during their weekly visit. They resisted her affections and glowered at her, seething with anger at the impossible pain she had put them through because of her addiction. Tears began to run down my face as I watched this little scene play out. I had to run out of the lunchroom because I was thinking of my own precious teenagers at home and how much I missed them. A couple of friends saw me run out and left their lunch to catch up with me. They didn't try and make it better. They just gave witness to the fact that I was hurting.

A place such as this levels the playing field. There is no richer, poorer, smarter, or prettier. Well, except for the Botox babes. After some of the women were at the treatment center a while, their fillers would begin to fail. Their facial skin started noticeably sagging. Other than that, there was no noticeable division of social class, age, education, or even gender. Just name tags with labels.

Pain decimates dividing lines, leaving stripped, exposed, raw veins of emotions. Pain is also a great equalizer. Pain had become too overwhelming, and life had become unmanageable for every one of us. It was such a relief to be with others who "got it" and who would allow you to grieve or struggle without placating.

I used to self-righteously comfort myself with the idea that I had always been accepting to people who are mentally ill. I had advocated for "their" meds and therapy. I have tried my best to be understanding and non-judgmental. Until I was the one who was staring a diagnosis in the face. The dawn of self-realization is like standing naked in a 360-degree dressing room with walls of mirrors and lights of judgment. Horrifying. The instant it dawned on me that I was struggling with mental illness, self-imposed judgment began swirling around me like Hitchcock's birds.

But now I understand more about mental illness. Life is an ocean of high and low emotional tides that roll in and out. Depression and anxiety are sneaker waves that suck at my daily life. I live in a disordered world where my unpredictable illness dictates the structure of my day. Mental illness is the Brach's mixed candy bag of undesirable things. I try dodging the past while balancing present and future, trying not to get caught up on any one of them. But every day I try to be grateful for the life I get to live.

4

Loaner Parents

I HAVE OBSERVED SEVERAL friends go through the arduous screening and tedious examination of their lives, to qualify to adopt a child. It is a deeply personal, thorough, deep dive into people's lives because giving a child to a family is a huge responsibility. Given their combined history, I have often wondered how in the hell my parents, Jay and Marilyn, passed that test.

My father, Jay, had a tragic upbringing, though it was shrouded in mystery. The only thing I remember hearing is that when he was young his parents used to drop him off at an orphanage when they were tired of him. They would pick him up when they felt guilty for leaving him. Repetitious abandonment.

His wife, Marilyn, my second adoptive mother, and the one with whom I spent the majority of my life, was born in 1940, almost exactly a year before the attack on Pearl Harbor. She was raised mostly in the south. She was the oldest of four brothers and four sisters. The facts I know about her life are sparse and even suspect, since she had a propensity for keeping the truth from us or misrepresenting it altogether.

The story relayed to me was that her family were migrant farm workers. They would travel from Missouri (colloquially pronounced Missoura) to California in the back of pickups. They picked crops through the summer season and then headed north to the Washington apple valley and picked there in the fall. Once winter hit, they headed home.

There were a series of stepfathers who wandered through their lives, but none went the distance. Marilyn reported that one stepfather was a mean, drunk, Blackfoot Indian. Because of him I believe she harbored bitterness against Native Americans for the rest of her life.

Marilyn told me she was raped by a stepfather. After that she slept with a knife under her pillow to keep it from happening to her again and to protect her sisters. Also, she told me she was horse whipped and run over with a tractor. She gave no more comments on these traumatic events. Only those facts.

Marilyn told me they were very poor, with little privilege and even less opportunity to rise above where they found themselves. She had an eighth-grade education.

As a child, I felt sad for her lost childhood and couldn't imagine the atrocities she endured. I almost didn't want to fault her for raising us the way she did, because she didn't know any better. On the other hand, because she was raised in a violent, chaotic, unstable household, I expected her to have known that she should do better.

I don't know when Marilyn met Jay, their love story, or how they came to adopt children. I don't know if they couldn't have children or if she didn't want to bear her own. Marilyn was fastidious about her body. She took pride in being tall and thin. At one time she had worked as a model, so her figure was very important to her. More than once the thought crossed my mind that perhaps she didn't want to get pregnant because it would ruin her figure. Mere speculation.

They divorced when I was four years old. We left Reno, Nevada, and headed north, landing in the Idaho panhandle, in Coeur d'Alene.

Marilyn was the champion of holding grudges. Early on in our time in north Idaho, in the mid-1970s, we went to a Payless shoe store. They wouldn't accept a check from her for some reason. We left the store with her yelling she would never darken their doors again. For the entire next decade she refused to go in there because of that one incident. She had the ability to stay mad at people for decades. She had siblings she didn't talk to and even cut off her own mother for a time.

She was Southern in nature. Everything had to appear externally "just right." I received an outfit once that had woolen shorts, a blousey rayon/cotton shirt, and a jersey knit jacket. She didn't like me wearing it because the fabrics weren't "right" together. We couldn't wear white until after Memorial Day and not after Labor Day. We weren't allowed to wear black because it made us look too grown up. We wore slips under every dress, never wore open-toed shoes to church, usually wore tights or pantyhose, and dressed up for the doctor, airplane rides (of which there weren't many), and all other professional appointments. We had clean underwear at the ready, should we ever need it in an emergency. We ironed bedsheets, dish towels, T-shirts, basically anything that could wrinkle. I ironed for hours—I was good at it. I even had a job ironing for a lady while in junior high. And the cardinal rule of looking "put together"? Have good shoes and a good bag—words I still live by.

She was only close to one sister throughout her life. Apparently there were seasons where her other sisters—Twila, Verla, and Elizabeth—were friendly with her, but it was Minda that she truly loved. Aunt Minda and her family visited us a few times in Coeur d'Alene. It was fun to feel like we were part of a larger family, besides just the four of us. My uncles—Neldon, George, Lester, and John—were, I think, truck drivers. One of them drove a load through north Idaho and we got to meet him. Before seventh grade, that is the only sibling I met, besides Aunt Minda. I don't even remember which uncle it was!

In 1984, just after school let out for the summer, Marilyn married Sandy, my awesome stepdad. He was larger than life. Loving, attentive, and jolly. I adored him, and he felt the same about me. His youngest was in high school, and I know he missed having little kids around. We had a lot of fun together. But by that fall Marilyn left Sandy for the first time. We packed up and headed to Missouri, where I started the seventh grade. While there, I met my cousins and aunts and uncles and my grandmother for the first time. There were so many relatives it was dizzying. Most of them lived in trailer homes on dirty lots.

I only spent time with my grandmother Minnie twice. Minnie was born with a short left arm. The arm was skinny, with a couple of finger-like extrusions and was vice strong. She seemed small and frail but had a combative strength to her. I wouldn't cross her for anything in the world!

One day, before my senior year of high school, on my second visit to Missouri, my grandmother came running into the hot, humid trailer home, grabbed a rifle, and ran back outside. I looked out just in time to see her kill a snake almost as long as I am tall. She gave the five-foot black snake, or "nope-rope," to the big dogs to play with. I wanted to throw up.

My aunts were expert and excessive southern cooks. Homemade biscuits and sausage gravy, hash browns, fried chicken, and sweet tea, the wine of the south, were all delicious.

However delicious the food, I hated Missouri. The snakes in the tepid lakes so warm they weren't even refreshing to swim in were horrible. The humidity was so thick you felt as if you needed a shower as soon as you got out of the shower. I didn't understand some of the Missouri drawl and they sure did not understand my northern accent. Words like "you'uns, we'uns and us'uns" were unfamiliar and just plain odd. To me, the only slightly enchanting thing about Missouri were the lightning bugs. They were fun to watch, trap, and play with. They almost made the sticky, hot evening skies magical.

Marilyn and Jay were carrying the heavy burden and stain of abuse, trauma, and neglect they had suffered. But this is what I know: abuse doesn't have to be a generational curse. When we know better, we should do better. And they did not.

5

The Yellow Rope

My family was sick. We were rife with secrets. From a very young age I understood that there were two faces of the family—one for public and one for private. In private, there was sexual abuse, physical abuse, and emotional abuse. In public we were bright smiling faces. The perfect church-going, hard-working American family.

My therapist said "secrets make you sick." I know this to be true. Secrets are a cancer that infects the family system, allowing it to become a petri dish of its own illness. That cancer spreads from person to person like recycled air on an airplane. Secrets thrive in a closed system like rotten poisonous mushrooms on a dark forest floor.

Jay was my father. The memories I have of him are difficult. I have carried shame for decades at what transpired. Blaming myself seemed a better alternative than blaming an adult who adopted us. Jay appeared to have wanted us, which makes the sexual abuse so hard to fathom.

Jay raped my sister, Dana' (pronounced Danay)—sodomized her, made her have sex with animals. Disgusting things that we only found out about in her thirties.

I remember his office. He was the head of the Chamber of Commerce for Reno, Nevada. He was the head of the church board. He was also a pornographic photographer. I have loathsome memories of his photography studio. He photographed adults and, based on my memories, I can only surmise he photographed children as well as adults.

Post-Traumatic Faith

My memories are hazy, yet sharp. Fuzzy, but clear. I see the room where the five of us were. Three men, Jay, and four-year-old me. We are in a make-shift photography studio. One man with a big belly has a dirty white T-shirt on. Another has a blue polo-shirt on over his blue jeans. Another man lurks in the shadows, but I know he is there. I know Jay is there but I can't see him.

My eyes scrutinize the room from the ceiling from where I am watching the events unfold. Against the backdrop of a red velvet curtain I am lying on a cold metal table. It looks to me like the kind of table you find in an industrial kitchen. I see a camera on a tripod. The dissociation causes the room to come in and out of focus. Black vignetting around the edges of my sight threatens to darken my view completely. And then, there is only feeling. Something cold, hard enters me vaginally. There is so much searing pain. I do not cry. Do not react. I have no faculties to protect me. And then, black.

The incident with Jay was repeated more than once. Mercifully, my brain has hidden some of the memories of the repetitive abuse through dissociation. Small flickers of memory frighten me awake at night. It wasn't until the hospital ran their battery of tests that I began to remember all that had transpired—and it almost sank me.

I'm not sure how Marilyn knew of the abuse, but signs point to the fact that she did. In an oddly protective streak, Marilyn divorced Jay to get my sister and me away from him. In 1977, she traveled to north Idaho, on her way to Canada, to get us from his grasp. However, she had friends in Coeur d'Alene, so we stayed there. I lived in north Idaho until I graduated high school in 1990.

On that day, the chair sat in the corner, the only thing I clearly remember the day we left Jay and Reno behind in 1976 was the chair. Its densely patterned brocaded fabric was the green hue of the seventies, registering somewhere between the nauseating color of pea soup and overripe avocados. The raised pattern was fuzzy and itchy to the touch. My finger would trace the patterns. Swirl, skip, swoop, jump. That chair may have been beautiful. I don't know. I just know it was his. I don't remember sitting together in it reading the funny papers or books. However, the presence of the chair hints at his presence in the house.

The Yellow Rope

The chair sat in the corner, surrounded by boxes, dwarfed by the empty room. Small and forgettable. Some days I imagine what was in those boxes. What precious mementos earned that honored place next to the chair? He was a professional photographer, who occasionally took portraits of his own children, all dressed up in matching outfits. Maybe he had favorite images he had saved to look at later. Maybe he had explicit pictures of other children. We'll never know.

As we packed up to leave our house, the gathering of belongings in the corner just kept growing. A thin yellow plastic rope stood sentry around that pile of stuff that Jay would be keeping with him in Reno. Everything within the boundaries of that rope had place, permission to be there until he came and got it. The chair was staying. I had to leave. Despite the abuse he was the only father I had known and I felt I belonged with him. However, I was on the wrong side of the rope.

I am vividly aware that my arrival in that empty living room, staring at the pile in the corner, with my back to an open door, was not without cost and effort, presumably much more effort than the choosing of that chair. He chose to be my father. He bought me. Adoption is a fortified bond because it is intentional. I am a product of a bond that is supposed to be stronger than family. I belonged to him, but he let me go. I think I was at least as beautiful as the chair.

When I was little, even though he had hurt me, I used to fantasize that he was coming to rescue us. I mistakenly thought that since we shared a name, he would be invested in protecting me from Marilyn. I didn't yet know he wasn't that kind of man. He wasn't a brave defender who would shield my body and block her blows. He was a coward who was only a hero in his own obsessions, fantasies, and homemade adult movies.

I assume that after we left, traveling states away from him, he returned to get his damn chair. All I know is I never did make it to the other side of that rope. I wanted a father who wanted me. He didn't want me. He chose to keep the chair and all the things within the boundaries of that rope, which didn't include me.

Once we were in north Idaho I have crystal clear memories of being taken to a pediatrician's office in a round, brown-paneled building near the hospital for an exam. A full pelvic exam was administered. I didn't know what was happening, only that the doctor's fingers were everywhere and inside of me. I was confused. Marilyn sat in a chair watching it all, smiling at me. For the next decade, every time we drove past those buildings, I panicked, and my stomach curdled.

Between the time of their divorce and my senior year of high school, I saw Jay twice. He visited once before kindergarten. He took me to play in the streams running through the rocks above the beach. During my seventh-grade year he came to visit again. We were living with my stepdad, Sandy, and Marilyn was so mad that Jay was there that she kicked a chair and broke two toes. Together Jay, Dana', Park, and I drove north an hour to Sandpoint to hang out in the restaurants and shops that were on the Cedar Street bridge. I have one picture of us there.

In 1990, while I was in foster care, the courts made an initial attempt to reunify me with my adoptive mother, Marilyn. Dana' sent me money so I could run away from the foster home. I flew to meet her in the Bay Area, San Francisco. At that time, Dana' was close with Jay and his long-term girlfriend, Betty, whom we adored. The tsunami of memories of the abuse he inflicted on us hadn't come yet to shore. So, even though I felt awkward around him, I just chalked that up to not having seen him much. I stayed with them for two weeks before I was forced to return to the foster home. I had hopes that we could build some kind of relationship out of the thin air of abandonment.

In 1999, Jay walked out of our lives forever when he found out we knew about the abuse. He went northeast from Reno and baked his hard heart in the Midwestern sun. We would never hear from him again.

I was afraid nobody would believe me if I told them what our home life was really like. I was ashamed of who I was and of what they had done. We looked amazing from the exterior, a beautiful mirage of good manners and accomplishments. Unfortunately, the interior of our lives was a hoarder's den of deep secrets, carried guilt, and garbage collected over past generations. So much useless, dangerous clutter. I learned how to keep the truth hidden even from myself. My dissociative disorder protected me by blocking so many painful memories. When those memories surface, they threaten my ability to cope, so I push them back down.

One of my first memories in the home of Jay and Marilyn Llafet is of my brother, sister, and I huddled underneath my crib while our parents yelled and screamed at each other. I am told their divorce was a shock to everybody who knew them. Those three kids under the crib, having been subjected to Jay and Marilyn's domestic war, were far less surprised.

6

Oldest

In 1976, we lived in a light-green two-bedroom duplex in Indian Meadows, on the west side of Coeur d'Alene, Idaho. The yard was unmanicured, as there were construction projects going on around us. This produced the most wonderful dirt piles. I dug, slid, and tunneled my way through hours of happy free time.

One of the earliest memories I have of my oldest sibling, Park, is from that home. Park was subjected to an experiment Marilyn found in a magazine. She had discovered a method of cutting men's hair that involved rubber bands. Different colored bands were placed in varying height pony tails throughout his hair. In theory, the hair would be cut at the bands and come out looking clean and tidy. Young though I was, I clearly remember rolling on the floor, laughing at him with pigtails all over his head. I can't be sure but I think the experiment was a bust. However, it did provide some merriment to that hot, stuffy apartment.

When she left, Marilyn always put Dana' in charge, even though Park was older. Park resented the usurping of his status as the oldest, and I resented my sister's dictatorial demeanor. My brother was my best ally growing up. He and I were conjoined in our dislike of her. We were a two-person mob, colluding with one another to beat Dana' at whatever game we were playing, usually outright cheating to gain any advantage we could. We played Battleship, Monopoly, and Sorry fast and loose. The money exchanged hands and was hidden with as much skill as any crooked dealer in Vegas could possess. There was no way she could fend off the both of us.

A natural artist, Park spent hours at his drafting table, drawing impressive house plans, cars, and interesting architecture. He consumed books about Frank Lloyd Wright and other favorite architects. Park had a ball made out of rubber bands that he would hurl at me to keep me out of his room if I tried to enter uninvited.

Park's passion was music. A very accomplished pianist, he played with enthusiasm and power. There wasn't much he couldn't play. Our teacher, JoElla, said he would turn the classical composers over in their graves with the way he "interpreted" their music. Park played with so much vigor that he managed to break two piano strings on our old Baldwin spinet. Those strings became prized possessions to him.

For years Marilyn worked as a personal caretaker for a woman with a physical disability. She would come home in the mornings to see us up and off to school, returning to work shortly before I left to walk to school. Then she would come home around 5 p.m. to make dinner, leaving again around 8 p.m. After she left for work, the power struggle between my siblings began, frequently ending in shouting matches. The fights were most often over Park's late night piano playing, which kept us awake. The large air vents in our old house, designed to let hot air flow upward from the basement wood stove through the house, were excellent communication tools. We would yell from upstairs, through the air vents, at him to stop playing so we could go to sleep, which generally yielded no response.

When he was in junior high, I heard a fight between Park and Marilyn. I was confused when it stopped abruptly. Shortly after that fight I saw a large purple bruise on Marilyn's hip, at her bed frame height. I surmised that he had pushed her and that stopped the fight. After that she didn't seem to beat up on him much.

Park loved clothes. He wore fitted pants, silky shirts, shiny suits, and zippered ties, all the rage in the eighties.

Park got older and started working. He mowed lawns all around the neighborhood. A hard worker, he dragged his mower behind his ten-speed bike for hours, getting blackened by the summer sun. I'll never understand why he worked so hard since every cent we earned was deposited into our bank accounts. We could deposit but it took her signature and ours to withdraw money, which we never were allowed to do.

Oldest

We all worked hard. Dana' worked at Arby's, slinging fries and roast beef throughout high school. I taught piano lessons during the summer from junior high school until I graduated. I was always embarrassed when Marilyn asked the church for scholarships to camps, retreats, and other events. We had money in the bank, but she just wouldn't use it. Our spending money was whatever Jay gave us at Christmas and birthdays. It started out as $25 and then was raised to $50. We stretched that out and made it last for months.

Eventually, in the early nineties, after she had disowned us all, Marilyn used that money to buy a house.

When Park was in high school, he and Marilyn started to verbally fight more often. Shortly after he graduated high school, he and I were in the basement family room in Sandy's house. A fight ensued and she picked up the paddles from an old-fashioned butter churn that were sitting as decoration. She beat him savagely with those large wooden paddles. After that she kicked him out of the house.

Years later I would learn that she called around to all our friends and church acquaintances. She asked everybody to not give him a place to sleep or food, or even talk to him. He "needed to learn a lesson." A close friend, grandmother type, told me she took him food because he was starving to death in the cold, moldy room that he rented in someone's house. I imagine him young, desperate, and hungry and wonder what he did or said to prompt her practically starving him to death. She didn't talk to him for some time. Years. We weren't allowed to communicate with him either. How lonely he must have been.

Later he moved in with friends. I recall him living with his friend in a white building with brown ginger breading on it. He tried college out at North Idaho College, the junior college in town, but he quit before completing. Despite a lack of formal education, he was always a consummate learner and avid reader.

I was shocked when, after thirty-one years of not talking to us, Marilyn left Park and me money in her will. It was an unexpected but appreciated gift. While I felt okay taking the money, since she had specifically left it for us, it did feel like a piss-poor substitute for losing thirty years of her in my life.

7

Beautiful Ball of Nothing

THE FIRST TIME I heard post-traumatic stress disorder (PTSD) mentioned was my freshman year of college near Seattle, Washington, in 1990. I was very sick. I could hardly eat anything except bread and water and wasn't sleeping. I found a doctor in Bellevue, Washington. He was inquisitive and thorough. Based on all the trauma that had transpired the previous year, he told me I had post-traumatic stress disorder. I had no idea what PTSD meant or what effects I was feeling because of it. Given the fact that it was 1990 and PTSD wasn't well researched or supported yet, he had no recommendations, just an admonishment to take care of myself!

In 2015, while at the hospital, I finally received a diagnosis of complex-PTSD (C-PTSD). It was actually a relief because somebody could finally describe to me what was going on with my brain and emotions. I am high functioning in my illness and have been fortunate to have lived a really amazing life, with lots left to live. I have also had great resources and support systems. God has been so good to me, and I can see his hand on my life and my days. But this is still a challenging diagnosis to live with.

One of the very real struggles of C-PTSD can be sleep deprivation. Because my nervous system is running on hyper-drive all the time, my body struggles to relax and rest. This happens even when I'm not aware of what is causing the anxiety. After years of insomnia I finally found meds to help me sleep, which is amazing.

C-PTSD nightmares gripped me for decades. I would wake up fighting my husband, who only had an arm around me in his sleep. Sometimes, in my sleep, I would have vivid flashbacks of abuse and wake up panicked and drenched in sweat. My monsters were real, and I never outgrew them.

These nightmares are among the most loathsome symptoms of C-PTSD. It would be lovely to lay down and rest without worrying about what ghosties may shake me awake in the night. Thanks to medication that calms the nightmares down, I no longer wake up terrified.

C-PTSD is a severe, but completely normal, reaction to abnormal, repeated trauma. It can be very isolating and exhausting. I've heard it referred to as the psychiatric equivalent of cancer. It has affected every part of my life, and often, because problems seem magnified in intensity, the decisions can be paralyzing.

C-PTSD affects every relationship I have—with my husband, my children, my friends. It whispers in my ear that I shouldn't trust anybody and reminds me that every time I do, I will get hurt. The cost is too high.

Complex-PTSD does not "heal" or "go away." However, with help a victim can learn to avoid triggers and manage the symptoms. It requires specialized, professional therapy.

I talked with a friend recently who was also diagnosed with complex-PTSD. She had been discharged from the hospital and was trying to figure out what life is like now on the "outside." We commiserated about symptoms, physical limitations, and frustrations. It felt as if we were speaking a special coded language that only the two of us could understand. Private language, like twins, with insider references and nonverbal understandings.

Mental illness can be so isolating! There are no bandages or braces to indicate that something is broken. Those of us with depression, anxiety, OCD, PTSD, or other mental-health challenges don't have anything to signify we are ill except for an occasional emotional breakdown. I don't walk with a cane or limp, and yet I need compassion even though I don't appear infirm.

To add to the complication, mental health is not an exact science. There are few accurate measurements to indicate whether one is in good mental health or not. It is a relative science filled with opinion, conjecture, and circumstance. Physical, mental, medicinal, hormonal, emotional, and spiritual factors are an ever-changing landscape. Together they create a giant game of internal Jenga. One never knows when one of those factors will cause unsteadiness and topple the whole tower.

Part of learning to live with C-PTSD is recognizing your own emotions. I've spent my life in public service and try to weigh and balance my words with wisdom. Therefore I have spent a lot of time biting my tongue and stifling my anger. I'm the pastor whose parishioners were going to start a blog entitled "Shit My Pastor Says," but I really did and do try and behave myself.

In spite of it all, none of us wants to be judged as over-sensitive, dramatic, or making up a symptom. We just want a chance to be honest about where we are in our quest for health and balance, hoping to find grace from those who love us.

A door slam, a twig snap, a weird sideways glance, a chair screeching across the floor, somebody standing too close, jostling, or someone's explosive anger—all triggers.

My heart races. I start sweating. Eyes race back and forth looking for an exit in case I need it. Hands tensing. Muscles twitching and taut. I try to think clearly. Consider what I need to do, say, or throw to get away. What is the quickest route to safety? Play and replay conversations in my head of how to end relationship, terminate conversation, leave.

I don't have the ability to consider whether or not you are here to hurt me. History and instinct tell me that is a certainty. I will protect myself at all costs. This is my C-PTSD.

There was one childhood home that I have particularly fond memories of. The big, yellow house with the farmhouse porch sat on the corner of 2nd and Roosevelt. It was walking distance to the lake, our favorite donut shop, and our favorite Mexican restaurant. I loved the garage of this house. It was small, brick red, and had a wonderful peaked roof that looked like it hid a mystery in its ample attic space.

The white, trimmed windows gave it a rustic barn-like appearance. On the outside was a lean-to shelter, with a fence around it that held my Easter duckies and chickens one year. I could climb the fence of that pen, shimmy up the lean-to roof, and sit on top of the garage, perched like the king of the hill. From this perfect location I could see our little gardens, my tire swing, and the back of our picturesque house. My climbing tree outside my bedroom window peeked at me from around the corner of the house. From this vantage point, if you stretched real tall you could see the fireworks as they lit off the lake on the Fourth of July. Some years, when my mother was working a night shift, my brother, sister, and I watched from there instead of from the downtown park.

For years that tiny one-car garage held a little secret in its musty, dingy space. Inside the garage there was a Gold 'n Soft butter tub that sat on a semi-hidden shelf. Inside was the most perfectly formed, symmetrical mud ball ever created. Just large enough to be cupped by my hands, it was my treasure. With great care year after year I formed, molded, grew, and, dare I say, loved that ball.

How could I love that ball of dirt? It didn't do any of the things a "good ball" should. There was no possibility of bouncing it or kicking it. You can't even hardly throw a mud ball. The impact of a catch could shatter it. What good was it? The older I get the more I think I understand. The ball was made good in my eyes by the investment I had put into it—time, emotion, joy, vision, and care.

It's silly when I think about it now. A wad of mud. Nothing more. I forgot to get it when we moved. I'm certain the next owners of the house didn't stand in wonder and amazement at my creation. I am confident they threw it away with the rest of the trash.

Today, I am lucky enough to be sitting in the first-class cabin. A nice man served drinks on trays in real glass cups. Even though I drink from real glass at home this feels like a luxury on the airplane, because it is. First class is expensive, and if you are willing to pay for the extra butt space and cushy chairs, then lucky you! Today it is "lucky me" because being married to a pilot is not without its perks, like being upgraded to first class.

But I feel like an imposter. As passengers tug their luggage to the back cabin, I wonder if they look at me like "how come she gets to sit there? She doesn't look rich, famous, or important." I feel like they have X-ray vision into my checking account and know I only have $13 there. I'm sure they know my shoes are from a bargain bin.

Often when I reflect on my life I see nothing more than a mud ball. I was not like other girls I admired. I was awkward. While other girls passed pretty notes to each other in classes and doodled their names across their papers, I couldn't accomplish the pretty, flowery, handwriting that young ladies seemed to spend so much time developing. I drew triangles and boxes.

Post-Traumatic Faith

My wardrobe was from the thrift stores. One year I had $26 to spend on my clothes for the year. I rode my bicycle all over town, scouring every bargain bin in the second-hand stores, building a wardrobe from them. It was very on trend for 1986. Even though I had new-to-me clothes, I still felt more under-dressed and under-coiffed than my fellow junior highers. I had braces, with headgear, which inspired a particularly beautiful seventh grader to tell me I was "chewing like a cow." My tendency to keep my nose in books and my desire to avoid crowds made me feel like the plainest, most useless form of a girl ever created. I may have looked cute and trendy, but I was afraid everybody knew I was wearing last year's clothes.

My favorite find that year was a cotton navy blue and green plaid skirt with buttons down the front. I put it on one day for school, and Marilyn was angry that it was too short. I must have not given her the compliant response she wanted, and she picked me up and held me against the wall by the throat, screaming at me. I changed, got on the bus, and cried my way to school.

I felt like that ball of dirt. Useless and unlovely. It has taken me a lifetime, but now I know. I am what my Creator imagined, and that is beautiful. What was on the outside is what mattered most to me—it has taken me my whole life to figure out that I am worth something because of my character, not because of my clothes. I'm not an imposter in someone else's drama. I'm the main character, the star, in my own story.

Our society is so enraptured by the outer trappings of one another that we frequently don't bother to look at the soul. We enshroud our character in ornaments that are nothing more than paper scraps that will deteriorate with time and exposure to the elements of life. It's time we placed value on one another by our character not by our appearance or accumulation of stuff. But herein lies the challenge. Before we can appreciate a person's character and soul we have to get close enough to them to hear their hearts.

8

Middle

My sister was a rule follower, quiet and obedient. She was the peacemaker. Quintessential middle child. When she was little, she would not dare cross or talk back to Marilyn. In later years, she argued and debated her idealistic viewpoints ad nauseam. Her debate training from school dunked her into arguments way above her head with only her inflated confidence to keep her afloat.

In 1976, shortly after we moved to Idaho, I remember Marilyn beating my sister. Her infraction that day? My sister had become itchy during church and was fidgeting, which angered our mom. Marilyn was embarrassed by my sister's behavior, and that warranted a beating. I remember my thin nine-year-old sister bent over the old rocking chair in the living room, not crying out as Marilyn beat her back and buttocks with a belt. Dana' never cried. She took the pain, her tears and her anger buried deep inside. Repeatedly Marilyn stuck her with fierceness, as if she was trying to elicit a reaction. It seemed she would never stop.

Jesus watched all this happen. From his gilded, carved, framed visage above the piano, Jesus watched my sister get beaten because she was allergic to her wool sweater. Blond haired, bright blue-eyed Jesus smiled gently, draped in white robes. Radiance glowed from his perfect face, beckoning everybody to love him. I watched this injustice play out and was too scared to save her, but I wondered why Jesus didn't bother to save her from this pain and indignity? On that day, and for so many hurtful, anguishing days to come, Jesus was silent and still.

Dana' feigned "perfect" for Marilyn, better than Park or me. She was an excellent student, a semi-studious musician, and loved to read. Within minutes of Dana' entering a crowded room, a posse would gather around her. It was an automatic party when she appeared, and she was their queen. Petite, beautiful, shapely, smart. In the parts department I was always jealous of Dana' because she had boobs and wavy hair. I had thick, straight, dark hair that wouldn't take a curl and was as shapely as a baseball bat. Dana' was vivacious and full of life. She was a local beauty queen and expert debater. I looked up to her, and if she hadn't been so bossy, I might have idolized her.

Even though she was four years older, she was smaller than I was. Sometimes when we fought I would climb on her back and put her in a head lock. She would scratch me with her big, long, fingernails, and draw blood. Fair play I guess, since I had her pinned down.

I loved to hide her things. It was big entertainment to me to watch her hunt for her favorite items while fuming at me. The problem is I have a dissociative disorder, which allows me to forget things easily. I just thought I had a bad memory. I could never remember where I put her things. One year when she was in junior high she got new panties for Christmas. I hid them and promptly forgot where. Some months later Park had a high school buddy spend the night at our house. With gusto and a flourish, they flipped the rolled-up sleeping bag out in his bedroom and out flew all of Dana's panties. She was horrified, and I was delighted.

Dana' loved to play music by the Romantic composers. She played the absolutely slowest, dirge-like music known to man. She chose music by Debussy, Brahms, and Schumann that was boring enough to put a pillow to sleep. Give me a good march by Strauss or a rousing ragtime ditty by Joplin any day. I loved to play pieces that actually had a pulse.

During high school, my sister entered a beauty pageant. Marilyn found her a deep-purple satin dress at a thrift store and added some lace detail. I was so proud, watching her walk the stage. An experienced debater and speech competitor, Dana' did an interpretive reading for her talent and answered questions like a pro. She won the crown that night, and we spent the next year watching her open the large resort in town, ride in parades, and greet dignitaries.

Middle

Dana's life goal was to be a doctor. She dreamed of having a nanny and a personal chef. Her short stint at college was fun for her; however, she flunked out. She was well loved, and immensely enjoyed the friendships she made in college. Brilliant though she was, she just couldn't get her head around school. After her first year in college in southern Idaho at Northwest Nazarene University, she changed majors. When she told Marilyn she was changing her major from pre-med to communications, Marilyn responded with, "Now what am I going to tell my friends?!" This was the preamble to two years of not speaking to her because Dana' "was now an embarrassment" to Marilyn.

Dana' moved to New York City in her twenties, in the late 1990s. The first interview a nanny agency sent her on was for the famous actors Alec Baldwin and Kim Basinger. She turned that job down and took on a different, wealthy, influential family.

During that stage in her life Dana' started her quest to address her inner life by going to a therapist. Together they decided Dana's emotional problems called for more investigative care than he could provide. She elected to participate in some memory-retrieving treatment by hypnosis. Dana' went to California with dreams of emptying her brain of all the demons that haunted her and instead came away with more ghosts than she could wrangle. She uncovered memories that were terrifying and evil. They included sodomy, bestiality, and sexual assault as a little girl, at the hands of Jay. Exposing these atrocities punched the gas pedal on the downhill slide of her mental health. She failed to pursue life-saving mental health follow-up care, so the horrific memories poisoned the deep wells of her mind and emotions.

After she turned thirty, she moved down to Orlando. They were opening a new resort and she went to interview for a spot as the director of their kids' daytime program. She was pulled out of that interview and offered the head of marketing because they liked her so much. Up to that point in her life, the only things that girl had marketed were Arby's burgers and fancy dresses!

Eventually, Dana' went to work for World Vision, an international network of individuals and organizations working to alleviate the plight of the poor and oppressed around the world. She was the youngest executive ever for World Vision.

However, by the time she arrived in Florida, Dana' was already coming unglued. She had become addicted to her pain medications, granted because of a botched stomach surgery, during which she had part of her stomach removed. Her need for a quiet mind fueled her addiction. She began to numb herself out with drugs.

In 2002, Dana' got married on Monhegan Island, an artist and art-enthusiast paradise off the coast of Maine. She got married to Michael before a small crowd of friends and family in the old church that still had gaslit lanterns in it. Their reception was on the lawn of the big house with wine, bread, lobsters, and charcoal flatbed grills filled with butter-dipped roasted veggies. We stuffed ourselves sitting among the tiki torches, listening to the waves lapping at the edges of the shore. The dance party was in the white, one-room schoolhouse. It was special, delightful, and a moment we weren't sure was going to happen because of her health.

Shortly after getting married, her husband would describe their living room as a 1970s drug scene with pills and alcohol everywhere. She was catatonic for months at a time. She never remembered me calling. She became convinced the drugs didn't work and procured a pain management system implanted in her spine. When that didn't satiate, she returned to pain-management drugs. Narcotics and barbiturates by the truckloads.

It was barbaric the way the system took advantage of her desire for prescription drugs. I flew to Florida just to plead with the doctors to cut her off. I went to their offices, carrying gallon-sized Ziploc bags of pill bottles in one hand and medical power of attorney in the other. I insisted they look at the volume of medications she was taking—some of them double- and triple-dosed by surgeons, pain management doctors, and general practitioners. The doctors insisted they were supplying her what she needed. I called insurance companies and every one of her doctors repeatedly, trying to get them to lessen her meds, to no avail. I hold them partially responsible for her death.

When my brother's family and my family started having children, Dana' and her husband rushed headlong into aunt and uncle roles. They loved the six of our kids deeply and spoiled them rotten. When they were around, the holidays were filled with wonderful gifts and decadent deserts.

The summer of 2005, Dana' came to Montana after buying a summer home the previous summer in the tiny town of Nye. With a waterfall, and a turtle/fishing pond and close proximity to Custer National Park, it was a fun, lovely place for my children to spend the summer. During that time her drug addiction was in full swing. She managed to move in and get settled with a fair bit of mania and a lot of help from me. But once the house was

Middle

arranged, she sank back into her drugs. She crushed pills and poured them into a quart-size measuring cup with hot water to dissolve. So many pills. In addition to her own pills, Dana' went through a large children's bottle of Benadryl every third day. I have deep shame for helping her pour that drug sludge down her jejunostomy tube (j-tube) while she lay in bed, waiting for dreamless sleep. She assured me all the medication was prescribed by doctors, and I didn't question her. By the time we were finished pouring all the drugs directly into her stomach each night, she was catatonic. I would close the j-tube, wipe up spills, and cover her up.

Dana' became emaciated and gaunt. Her skin was dull and saggy. The effects of her addiction were no longer secret. Her body was telling her story. She became suicidal and anxiety ridden.

Sometime during that summer in Nye, out of nowhere, Dana' decided she no longer wanted to be married. She returned to Florida and cleaned out their house while her husband was at work, leaving him with no explanation and very few possessions from their household. Eventually she would say that he was the worst of her mother and father combined. Given the heinous nature of each parent, and after being an integral part of Michael and Dana's lives, that seemed hard to believe.

Park and I had a battle over whether Dana' was a drug addict. She quit talking to me because I told her she was an addict. It was so hard for him to see when he wasn't around to see her day-to-day. Luckily, after she went back to Florida, he flew down to see first-hand what was going on. Alarmed, he and her friends did an intervention. In a stroke of good sense, she deferred to the group and agreed to go back to Washington with him to enter rehab.

Three days into rehab in Washington, and she declared herself cured. According to her, she was the best patient they had ever had. She checked herself out, got on a plane, went back to Florida and got her car. We understood that she was going to make her way across the country and return to Vancouver, Washington, to live near my brother.

Days into her trip and nobody had heard from her. A month passed, and we filed a missing persons report. We were desperate to find her. The authorities found her in Texas, living with a random couple she had met at a bed and breakfast. They were so taken with her they invited her to live with them. She remained a de-facto part of their family until her death in 2015.

Dana' never re-engaged with us once she got to Texas. She wrote us off as relatives that didn't care about her. A stab to my heart, she sent Christmas letters to our family and friends about how wonderful it was to finally have a family to care for her when her own family had abandoned her.

Our battles notwithstanding, I always loved my sister but also have always been glad that, since we aren't biologically related, I'm not swimming in her gene pool.

Just before the ball dropped, crushing 2014 and welcoming 2015, at 11:50 p.m., the phone call that I had expected for ten years arrived from Texas. My sister—emaciated, sick, and drug-addicted—had succumbed. She was dead. In fact, she had been dead for hours. Those hours while we celebrated the end of the year and anticipated the next, she was dying. I had resigned myself to the knowledge that she would be alone and desperate in her death. I never imagined that she would die with friends and family by her side. The years of illness and addiction had hammered any hope out of me that she would die of natural causes. And there wasn't a damn thing I could do about it. So here we were. After a long period of addiction and self-imposed alienation, she died emaciated and alone in a filthy apartment in Texas. We eulogized her on her forty-sixth birthday in 2015.

I miss her terribly. But the truth is, I began accepting her death years before, when it became obvious how ill she was. She rejected the people who really loved her and wanted to help her heal: physically, emotionally, and mentally. She built an imaginary family who ignored her addictions and rejected reality from those who loved her and tried to tell them. Her new, fabled life embalmed her from real feelings and from truth. My fear about going to a workshop on childhood trauma was that I would fall prey to the same demons she had unearthed. I feared I would become like her.

Nothing redeems the fact that I have no sister, and except in the case of my catastrophic demise, I will be the last of my family alive. Sobering. Real. Truth. Sometimes I hate the truth. I wear her diamond star around my neck and think of her daily.

10/15/15
Dana',

> *I never expected to write you a letter you could not receive or read. I always hoped there would be one more chance for us to talk.*
>
> *I imagine you dying alone, and I wonder if you left the earth with anger and hatred or with peace. I hope the latter but fear the first, because the drugs drove you to become a different person than I knew.*

Middle

The person I knew was vibrant and strong. She loved life and it loved her. She tried desperately to love the world and yet now I know you didn't love yourself.

I am sad for you. For all the suffering and pain that you lived with the entirety of your life. You deserved more and I'm sad you never saw it materialize.

I just wanted to be part of your world and life. You took that from me. Now my family is smaller and emptier without you in it.

9

Living in Church

ALL MY LIFE I have been in church. As a child, every time the doors were open, our family was there. Jay was the head of the church board. Marilyn was the church secretary. Some of my earliest memories are of the church, Sunday school rooms, and playing in the nursery while Marilyn worked. I remember tearing up bits of paper to make pretend cookies to serve alongside the little pink plastic teacups. Not tall enough to reach the light switches, I played with sunlight illuminating the table. In the sanctuary the dark wood pews were familiar and soothing. It felt as much like home as any place could have for an orphan new to the country.

As I grew older, my fondness for the church grew. I enjoyed it even when we were there six days a week. Five days for private school and one day for church. My best friend Michael was there, and I accepted the surroundings as normal.

When in private school, second through fourth grade, we sat in cubicles facing the walls with large white particle-board dividers between each child. We worked in small magazine-sized lesson books, a different book for each subject.

One day in the second grade, we were learning about punctuation. I copied the sentences dutifully but didn't notice that I was supposed to insert periods and commas. Each student checked their own work from a master text at a station in the center of the class. I checked my work and deemed it completed, again not noticing the punctuation. My teacher, Mrs.

Applebee, told Marilyn that I had cheated by marking my work correct. I was hauled up to the principal's office where he beat me with a large paddle with holes in it. When I got home, Marilyn said since I cheated she would remind me every day for the next week not to cheat. In our basement filled with canning and laundry, she bent me over the wooden steps and beat my bare backside with a large stick every morning before school for five days. I lived all day, every day of that week, dreading the next morning.

Still, some of my happiest memories were from church, perhaps because it was the only socialization we were allowed. I remember playing in the wheat growing on the prairie surrounding the church and sliding down dirt piles after school. I remember fall carnivals and birthday parties. I didn't even mind the navy blue and maroon, prairie-style uniforms the girls wore.

We got kicked out of that prairie church. They called it ex-communication. We were ostracized from our friends. They were forbidden to speak with us. I couldn't play with Michael or even speak to him anymore. Marilyn had sinned by dating a Jehovah's Witness man, Bob, warranting the ousting, since he was in a religion outside our faith. Bob was a neighbor who lived down the alley. I remember that his family didn't celebrate birthdays or holidays. His faith wouldn't allow that. He was a Jehovah's Witness. I decided that would be a dismal way to live and hoped our families wouldn't merge. In my mind's eye, I saw Christmas and my birthday slowly being thrown out with the garbage in the alley.

After Bob and my mother broke it off, he called the city authorities out of spite and told them about the Easter ducks and chickens Marilyn had bought me. The city cited us and instructed us to remove them. Damn him and his uncelebrated existence.

We joined another church where the rules were less rigorous. Women wore pants to church, and teenagers wore blue jeans. I met the most glamorous women ever in the girls' club that met on Wednesday nights. They were beautiful and wore lovely makeup and jewelry. My Sunday school teacher, Charlotte, was tall, thin, and very old. Charlotte loved us a lot. She had a box of treats for successful memory-verse recitation and once a year held a whole class party at her trailer home. It was an honor, bestowed on each child in rotating order, to take the brown and orange Sunday school attendance books and tan offering envelope up to the Sunday school secretary for them to log in their ledgers.

Post-Traumatic Faith

The back of the stage in the sanctuary had white rock, floor to ceiling. During church, since I wasn't allowed to go to children's church, I used to draw the platform wall, stone by stone, until the closing song. I drew three-dimensional crosses like the one high on the wall, center stage, above the baptismal cove. Sometimes I would draw the criss-cross woodwork, high in the center of the room, where the sunlight was allowed in through the skylight windows.

I have such sharp and vivid memories of that church. I clearly remember ending church services singing the Lord's prayer, with its high F, which many would aspire to and few would achieve. I clearly remember the stately Pastor Robinson with his salt and pepper hair. I loved Pastor Jim Hance, with his shock of poofy, strawberry-blond hair.

It was at this church that I met my one and only youth pastor, Tim. Tim was fun and dedicated. He and his wife hauled us all over to camps, winter snow/ski retreats, summer camps, and weekly Taco Bell outings. We went to Pizza Hut, until we were invited to never go back there, and Dairy Queen. I would buy the very cheapest thing on the menu, sometimes just water, trying to make my paltry Christmas and birthday money last throughout the year. We played softball and hosted Valentine's Day pasta dinners, had game nights and all-night New Year's Eve sleepovers. Being north Idaho, even the poor kids could ski and swim. So, we spent winters on the ski hill and summers on the lake.

Most importantly, I remember spending the hour before our service praying for our time together. I remember a band of young adults dedicated to seeing the message of Jesus moving forward into our community. The group grew. It was the first time I saw the power of prayer move people into action and response so tangibly.

Youth gatherings were my approved social events, and I treasured them. But even at youth group I was on my guard. I never shared anything deeply personal for fear of Marilyn finding out. For the love of all that is holy, even when we were praying in regular church services, she wanted to know what we were praying about. Nothing was sacrosanct, including our communique with God.

In 1989, I went on a mission trip to Mexico where we worked in the dirtiest of slums, with their open sewers flowing down the street. We worked with children, presenting dramas in open air, communicating the gospel across cultural boundaries. However, when I returned, Marilyn did not travel to pick me up in Seattle like the other parents. She had the other moms take care of me until I reached home. I was simultaneously disappointed and relieved she didn't come.

Once home, I stood in the shower and cried. I cried because for the first time I realized my privilege. I had a sparkly, clean shower and bathroom where I had warm water to get clean. And I cried because I felt trapped. I had returned home, where I was once again unsafe, even more than I had been in the Mexico slums.

※ ※

At the hospital in Arizona, in 2015, there was a worn-out old list on the bulletin board of churches that would send a van to pick us up for services. The only problem was we weren't allowed off campus for the first few weeks. My other problem was that I was in such deep grief that I couldn't be with *my* church and *my* people. To go to another church made me feel like a new widow who was being asked to date. I couldn't stomach the thought.

After spending almost every day of my life in church, it would be six years before I would re-engage with a church on a regular basis. I couldn't bring myself to participate in corporate worship. I was heartbroken.

Six years without the life raft and ritual of church; I was adrift, waiting for my health to catch up with my hope. I have had to remind myself that going to church doesn't equal faith. That season re-prioritized my relationship with God to be what it always should have been—focused on Christ, not on the gathering of people. I can now focus not on what I have lost, but what I have found—my personal expression of faith.

※ ※

I really don't understand parades, but I love them. However, you stand outside in the heat, cold, and/or rain watching other people walk by and wave. Growing up in a small town, we went to every local parade. I loved seeing people I knew on the floats, marching bands, and old classic cars. It was always loud, crazy, and fun. I love it so much we tune into the Macy's Thanksgiving Day Parade every year and enjoy it from our living room over cinnamon rolls!

It occurs to me that parade culture is a unique convergence where the participants need the observers just as much as the observers need them, for the whole idea to succeed. A parade without anybody cheering, clapping, enjoying is an awkward, solitary walk.

So, I'm mentally throwing my own parade. I'm sitting and waving with gusto and in support of my friends and family who are working hard at keeping the church moving forward in grace, justice, and wisdom. And I'm praying too. Waving and praying. This is my way of participating in the streams of life that I'm not quite "in the flow" of. And I know they need my support as much as I need theirs. So keep on marching, friends. Keep marching.

And relax, people. My not going to church does not mean I'm going to hell—just to Starbucks.

10

Sandy

In 1984, when I completed the sixth grade, Marilyn met and married a man I adored. My tall, bald, jolly stepfather, Sandy, was so much fun. He allowed me to ride with him on the school bus route he drove around the east end of the lake. At the end of the year, he would let the kids have a whipped-cream fight on the bus. Sandy was also a realtor. He and I would paint his bright yellow signposts and pound them in the yards of houses he was selling. He hung a tire swing in the tree in the yard and allowed me to make the hot tub room into Barbie paradise. My garage sale Barbie houses, pools, and yachts surrounded the empty hot tub. I stood in the middle and orchestrated their world for hours. He loved to grill and cook. His signature dish was hamburgers baked in mushroom soup gravy. You would have thought he served up a four-course professional meal with all the pride he displayed in that specialty dish. When I was with him, I felt safe and adored.

My stepdad fixed up motor bikes for me so I could ride the trails across the street from the house. The unsupervised freedom was delicious. I rode to my heart's content. There was a fable that somebody had strung piano wire across one of "my" trails, to keep the motorcyclists from riding there, and it had decapitated one kid. I always tucked my chin close to my chest when I passed that point, just in case the rumor was true.

Sandy was almost as Catholic as the pope. A picture of John F. Kennedy Jr., American Catholics' poster boy, hung in the center of the family picture wall. On Sundays, we went to mass with Sandy and then went to the Pentecostal church. I loved the icons and the grandeur of Catholicism. I knew enough about faith to appreciate the traditions around the sacraments. The regular reading of Scripture and the reverence attended to it impressed me. My love of liturgy and tradition, which began in the seventh grade, would pop up later in my own church.

One summer day I had been out riding my bicycle. When I returned home, I put my bike in the garage, but not in its specific parking space. I went inside and promptly forgot about it. When Marilyn returned home from work and the bicycle infringed on her parking space, she lost whatever little cool she had. She came in the house raging and sent me to my room. She followed me there and proceeded to beat me. Because I wouldn't comply and just bend over the bed so she could beat me with a belt she began to hit me over and over. By the end of the beating I had two black eyes, my jaw hurt to open and shut, the ringing in both my ears was such that I could hardly hear. I had bruises and welts all over the rest of my body.

The worst part was that she confined me to my room, allowing nobody to see me, not even my brother or sister. Least of all the stepfather I thought would come to my defense.

I stayed in my room for close to two weeks, taking my meals there and only leaving to use the restroom. She would walk in silently, drop off my meals, and walk out without uttering a word. Besides her, the only life I saw those two weeks was two wild bunnies I could watch through my high, tiny basement window, playing in the yard. I envied their freedom.

My body was injured, and my pride, confidence, and security lay in bloody shreds and shambles. The loneliness I felt was not just the absence of people in my bedroom but also the absence of people participating in my rescue. Nobody came to look for me. Nobody cared that I didn't show up at church or school. As far as I could tell, nobody so much as inquired about me. I never understood why Sandy didn't save me or come to talk to me. He was home, and yet he let her beat me mercilessly. We never talked about it. And it all happened because I didn't put a bicycle in its proper spot.

As a small child I used to fantasize about running away. I wondered if people would feed me, if I could get a job to make money, and contemplated where I would live. All big problems for a small girl to consider, but they seemed reasonable questions to take on if I were to survive. Ultimately, I decided I couldn't survive without her, even if I doubted I would survive her. One of her mantras was, "If you run away, the police will come and put you in jail. I am *not* coming to get you." I believed her. Up until college I had an unreasonable fear of law enforcement. I was convinced they were coming to lock me up.

Sometimes my mind plays tricks on me. I think, "Yes, my mother was not a great mom." Minimizing her effects on me, "She was kind of bad." Because Marilyn told me that nobody would ever believe me if I told them what she did, I excused her actions and denied how truly terrifying she was. That way I could retain the feeling that I was a bad kid, and she was a good mom. I needed that insulation to survive and not go crazy. It wasn't until I was in the hospital that someone first uttered the words, "Jill! She was a sociopath."

In Sandy's house, the garage rafters held a fabulous secret. Always a writer, I couldn't help but put some of my thoughts and feelings down in words. I had a few diaries over the years, taking the risk they might be found. Sandy's big garage attic, filled with old snow machine clothing, holiday décor, and cobwebs of memories past, gave me ample space to store my diary. While it seems an extraordinary effort to climb up into that hot, steamy attic every time I wanted to hide my diary among the dusty boxes, it was worth it to minimize the risk of being caught with words that could incriminate Marilyn. I discovered an old cream and pink radio in the attic. I took it apart, hiding the parts in the attic and bringing the shell into my room. In it a small diary lay sequestered and silent. Over the years I hid my diary under mattresses, at school in my locker, in the attic, in the basement, and deep in dresser drawers. I imagine that her head would have exploded had she ever found one of them, but miraculously she never did. They are now resting beneath my graduation caps, tassels, stoles, certificates, and diplomas, my kids' baby memorabilia and notes, charts, and graphs from the hospital.

I have considered, more than once, destroying them, tossing them out like yesterday's news, but something compels me to keep them. Perhaps after this book is written I will silence their voices by fire or shredder. I just don't want future generations to read them and excavate horror or pain that isn't theirs to carry.

Post-Traumatic Faith

I have no knowledge, as is appropriate, of what caused Sandy and Marilyn to divorce. All I knew is that they fought a lot, and it was much more peaceful when they weren't together. I think they only managed to live together for no more than nine months during their two-year marriage. I remember wishing more than once that Marilyn would have let me stay with Sandy, but that wasn't an option. I was stuck with her.

11

Shared Space

My first roommate of memory, much to my chagrin, was my sister, Dana'. Dana' was a closeted messy person. I am not. She wasn't allowed to have things strewn about the room, but she successfully stuffed every drawer and niche with junk. I remember Marilyn dumping out all of her drawers on the floor to get Dana' to organize them. She never succeeded in coaxing the messy out of her though. As a married adult, Dana's house was different levels of dirty and messy, depending on what season her addiction was in.

My second roommate was in college. I walked into my first dorm room, carrying my light-blue striped comforter, blue towels, and typewriter. I had no presuppositions of what this roommate situation would be like, but like all freshman there was anxiety about whether we would get along.

What I found when I crossed the threshold was a sweet-faced girl with curled bangs that stood straight up about eight inches about her forehead. It was, after all, 1990. She sat criss-cross, leaning against the wall, on a homemade patchwork quilt. She had put posters of every current Christian rock band up on the wall. She had a rocker T-shirt and tight jeans on.

Considering I was never allowed to listen to Christian rock, the wild posters and rocker girl were a jolt to my senses. Marilyn loved to listen to golden oldies, forties and fifties-era music, set to orchestration, from her reproduction old stereo. It was as if I was being raised in a never-ending elevator soundtrack. The first cassette tape I remember seeing was by a band called the Imperials, which Marilyn hated. My sister played *The Trumpet of*

Jesus on repeat. According to Marilyn, Amy Grant was *probably* not going to send us to hell, and Sandi Patty was the queen of Christian music whose vocals soared along with her impeccable reputation, which lasted until she sinned by getting divorced. But rock music, Christian or not, was taboo.

My roommate, Donna, turned out to be the sweetest and gentlest of pals. She was one of those people who seemed fake, sickly sweet, but turned out to be the real deal, genuinely wonderful.

Being in a dorm room and taking care of myself shone a light on how embedded Marilyn's habits were in me. All the things in my drawers were placed in exacting rolls and squares. My school supplies and decorations had very specific places in the room. My friends used to tease me because I didn't leave the dorm room until my pencils were lined up in height order on my desk, printing side up. I ordered my world as rigidly as Marilyn did, trying to control the internal chaos by taming my environment.

After doing laundry one day, I thought I would try and break at least one of these crippling habits. I folded all my laundry and then, gasp, threw all my socks in the drawer without folding them or lining them up in the drawer like crayons in a new box. I triumphantly went to bed. And then proceeded to lay awake until 3:00 a.m. All I could think about was those socks. I finally got up, arranged the drawer neatly, and dropped into peaceful sleep. Eventually my OCD lessened as I got more control of my world. Then I had four children, which completely buried the remnants of my OCD under the laundry, sippy cups, and cracker crumbs.

My next roommate was my husband, Kyle. The summer of 1992, I met Kyle from Billings, Montana. Frankly, I disliked him before I met him because I was sick of hearing about him. Several of my dorm mates had fallen for him. "He's so cute. He's so polite. He sings so well. He is so smart. Blah. Blah. Blah." Their incessant conversation about him wore me out. However, that summer we became friends. In September of 1992, we started dating, November we decided we wanted to be married, December we told our parents, January I had a ring, and July of 1993 we were married. It was a whirlwind, but I knew I had made a good decision and God had blessed me with a good man.

Living with somebody else and establishing my household was like playing house. We had a small two-bedroom apartment. We loved hosting people for games and food. The first year was bliss, with hardly a cross word between us. The second and third years, we fought like hostile roommates and made up like lovers. My early sexual trauma started to peek out during this season in the form of flashbacks, but I ignored them and kept working and going to school. I kept busy to stay away from my past and establish my future.

However, being only three years away from my mother's house, there was no way I could avoid bringing baggage into the relationship. I was insecure, authoritative, and anxious. I struggled with undiagnosed depression and complex-PTSD. We didn't know the depth of the mental and emotional challenges we were facing, but we soldiered on, making the best of young marriage.

And then there were new roommates. Tiny, squalling, beautiful bundles of joy and poop. Emily arrived in 1996. However, the strain of working such opposite schedules was taking a toll on us, so we decided to move to Montana for a couple of years, where we could get family support and get a little better established financially. We found out we were expecting Alexander as we were deciding on the move. Alexander came in 1998, Brittany in 1999, and Taryn in 2001.

At two years old, when Brittany was sick and miserable because of her childhood leukemia, often she would come to our room and climb into bed. A queen-sized bed feels small to my 6'1" husband, but add me and a toddler and it seemed impossibly small. Then Taryn started to walk. She would crawl out of her bed and bang on our door. "Mama! I want my Mama!" We were too tired to argue with her, so she would get to climb into our bed too. Occasionally Alex would join us. Three kids and two adults was beyond capacity for 60 x 80 inches of space.

I do love being a mom. People ask me frequently if it was chaos with so many little kids at once. I don't remember it being crazy, just busy. They turned our life upside down, but we gave everything we knew how to give to our parenting. We loved those little roommates but were glad they eventually reacclimated to their own beds. We are now enjoying watching them create spaces for their own families outside of our house!

My first roommate at the hospital was a beautiful black woman. Nicole sat cross-legged on the bed across from me and introduced herself. I don't remember our conversation, only that I felt comforted by her presence in my disconnected world. I do remember her saying, "You are a walking enigma—a cussing, down-to-earth pastor?" She welcomed me into a space where I felt like a foreigner. Nicole never did manage to outrun her demons and ended her life several years ago. I wish she hadn't felt so lost when she was the one who helped me feel found.

Because I stayed in a two-bed room, I would get new roommates regularly, which is unnerving not knowing who they were and what their issues might be. But I was always warned someone was coming and reassured of my safety. As roommates were cleared medically, they were released to the apartments to share rooms with one to three other people. However, due to my dissociative disorder, I was not allowed to move into the dorms, which were largely under-supervised. The nursing station, where I lived, was noisy, busy, and often tumultuous. But I felt safer there with an entire staff dedicated to keeping me safe from myself.

Laurie was the next roommate I remember. I walked into my darkened room, where Laurie was lying in bed crying, clutching a baby toy. Like me, she felt lost and confused. The concrete thing in her mind was that she missed her baby and knew she wouldn't see her for several weeks. Her anxiety was crippling. Even the slightest thing set her off. She watched me brush my teeth one night, and the vigor with which I was brushing almost threw her over the edge. However, she was a wonderful roommate and I enjoyed getting to know her.

Bianca came to stay with me for a couple of days, when she wasn't feeling safe alone in her dorm room. We were already friends, having bonded over our lack of addictions, which was very rare in the trauma hospital. The large majority of people with addictions are compensating for some trauma they have experienced, but neither she nor I had that added complication. We are still the truest and most loyal of friends.

Another roommate, Colleen, came from upstate New York. She was a wealthy woman, having led some of the hugest corporations in the nation. Just like the rest of us, she was simultaneously confused and relieved at being there. Her trauma was surfacing at a time when she was not working and was finally able to find the time to care for herself. She had tall, beautiful boots on with really long shoelaces. I wondered why they didn't take her laces away from her.

Shannon was shattered when she came to be my roommate. She had been assaulted—which is an inadequate way of saying she was raped—by a superior officer in the Marines. She was a kind, beautiful girl, and it hurt my heart to see her in so much pain. She didn't want to transfer to the dorms because it had stairwells, and she had been assaulted in a stairwell. Because of the rape, she had a pregnancy scare while being a patient at the hospital. I prayed she wasn't pregnant with her rapist's baby. Fortunately, the test was negative. Eventually, staff convinced her to go to the dorms, and I was once again by myself.

There were other roommates at the hospital—some of whom I don't remember due to dealing with my own trauma, but the ones I do remember were just like me: searching, confused, lost, and trying to find our place in a new-to-us world.

When I returned from the hospital, I really didn't want a roommate. I didn't want Kyle. I wanted to be left alone. I didn't want to be touched or held. I slept on the couches, on spare beds, anywhere I could to not have to sleep with him. It took a year before I decided I could sleep with him again, and occasionally I still feel that same way, like I don't want to be touched for fear of being hurt by one of the evil ghosts, memories without flesh and blood.

12

Meeting the Aryan Nations

I GREW UP IN the Aryan Nations–infested north Idaho of the seventies and eighties. The Aryans established their twenty-acre headquarters a few miles north of Coeur d'Alene in 1974 and remained until 2001. Their ultimate goal was to take over the Pacific Northwest, creating a white homeland for themselves. Their faithful marched around their compound with weapons, daring anybody to tangle with them. The lack of diversity in the area paled in comparison to other parts of the country. People of color either fled or avoided that part of the Pacific Northwest entirely. We had a friend who was a retired Los Angeles police officer. Since he was a black man, he didn't feel comfortable going out in public unless he had his gun vest on.

Led by Richard Butler, the white supremacist group created chaos in the area for decades. When I was a child, we lived on 2nd and Roosevelt, near downtown. I remember hearing the boom from bombs being set off at the local bank. I recall the burning of a cross on a local Jewish realtor's front lawn. The skinheads, a branch of the Neo-Nazis, held parades through downtown, with men in sheets and hoods. The group attempted to firebomb a local priest who was a diversity advocate. They chased down and beat a Native American woman and son, which led to their ultimate demise. The family won a huge lawsuit against them, and the Aryan Nations was forced to declare bankruptcy, losing their property, influence, and financial backing.

In an attempt to reverse the image of the area as a region of hate, every year Martin Luther King Jr. Day was a huge celebration in Coeur d'Alene. The school children made flags, colored pictures, and did art projects that were displayed all over the local college campus. Our music festivals and speeches, all decrying the hatred and bigotry of the area, were nationally televised.

I graduated in a class of 550 students in 1990. We had fewer than five students of color in the class. There were three Asian students in that mix. As a Korean American, I was simultaneously conscious of standing out and of blending in. Our family was on the front page of the newspaper, showcasing the wonderful white woman raising three Korean orphans. However, to my friends, I was never treated as different, unique, or special. I was just me. Ethnic diversity was, curiously enough, not a huge conversation, because there really wasn't any to speak of. No one pointed out that I was different. I would never have thought of calling myself a Korean American. I do remember being called "Jap" and "Chink" in jest, terms for which I did not have historical knowledge or context, so I did not know to take offense.

The Reverend Richard Butler came into the steak house where I worked the summer of 1990. He, his wife, and bodyguard arrived one Sunday after the church crowd had left and before the dinner rush started. The restaurant was empty at that 3 o'clock hour. I was the host and greeted them and sat them at a booth. The dinner party neither acknowledged me nor made eye contact. When I went into the kitchen, the staff were saying things like, "If I had a gun I would go out and shoot him right now," all the while leaving me to serve the group. As they ate, I was cleaning a table in a section just above them, with only white wood lattice in between us. Whether their conversation was for my benefit or not, I heard it. Butler was talking about Asian pastors. He was saying how ashamed they should be for daring to share the gospel, given their non-Caucasian status. Of course, he had no way of knowing I was called to be a pastor and was passionate about the gospel. But God did. I think he allowed me to hear that conversation, which only solidified my determination to follow that career path.

I went to college in the highly diverse Seattle area where the ethnic groups naturally drifted together. The Korean community at school was tight and they accepted me as one of their own. They consistently told me I was "so Korean." I had no idea what that meant. However, in working with my first church, a Korean congregation, I found that even though I didn't speak the language, I fit in. Their homes were so comforting to me. I felt as if I could curl up on the couch and sleep or put my feet up on the coffee table. How could that be? I was raised white, in a white family, in a bleached white culture, so how could I think of myself as anything other than white? I didn't know if I should call myself Korean American, Korean, or American. It was so confusing that it took me years to come to the conclusion that I am, in fact, Korean American.

Marilyn wasn't particularly fond of black people and told me I could not ever marry a black man. I asked why and she would never give me a concrete reason for this. I believe she was racist, but she would have been furious if anybody had ever said that about her. After all, she did adopt three Asian children.

When I was in the sixth grade I did a research project on Korea. The crayoned South Korean flag graced the cover of my report. I remember at that time asking Marilyn about my birth family and country of origin. She told me it didn't matter, I was hers now. I wasn't encouraged to embrace or investigate my cultural heritage.

I often wonder if some of the conflict between Marilyn and us kids wasn't because the fundamental difference in our backgrounds. Some research supports the concept that babies in utero absorb emotional acceptance and understand more about their surroundings than we previously thought. It is generally agreed that the first months and years of a baby's life are crucially formative in their grasp of who they are and where they "belong." No matter the circumstances of my arrival, I was born into Korean culture and my first years were spent in Seoul. So, I wonder if any of our conflict could be attributed to our different upbringing. It's possible—it's also possible she was just mean.

In 1997, when my husband and I with our toddler daughter moved from the Seattle area to dramatically less diverse Montana, I worried about my children's future understanding of their diversity. I craved experiences for them that would expose them to their own cultural history and widespread acceptance of others. We did our best to provide that for them.

My experience at the very expensive hospital was also eye opening in terms of culture. The vast majority of those in attendance were very privileged Caucasians. Many of these people were trust fund babies. They talked about their cycle of regret, relapse, and repeat, and all the expensive rehabs they had been to. I heard conversations about whether or not to sell their third or fourth home. They had juggled the decision to go to Betty Ford or here. There was a disproportionate number of ethnic people compared to

Caucasians. I observed this while acknowledging the privilege that allowed me to be treated in such an elite institution. But I want the same privilege for others and wondered if there were other equitable treatment centers that were more diverse.

13

Basement Candy

I LIVED IN A basement when I was in junior high, 1985. Bare cement floors. Single bulbs hung here and there from the open joist ceiling. The light bounced off the shiny, foil-wrapped insulation stuffed between the studs of unfinished walls.

My sister's side of the basement had pretty, white, carved furniture with gold trim and a white, cast-iron, scrolled bed frame. My side of the room had left-over, used furniture, but a similar twin bed frame. Marilyn had scavenged the frames from somewhere and had them painted for us one Christmas.

On my side of the room, under the thin basement window, I had a white bookshelf. On it, amongst other things, was a glass jar filled with hard candies. The strawberry candies wrapped to look like the berry, butterscotch candy, and individually wrapped lifesavers were my favorites. Treats were a high commodity, so I hoarded mine. Occasionally, when I got mad at Marilyn, I went downstairs and ate a piece of candy to make myself calm down and feel better. It placated me some since I certainly could not show my emotion without fear of being beaten.

One Saturday after yet another fight with Marilyn, I fled to my basement bedroom. With tears drowning my face, I wondered how I could continue to live like this. As I sat on the cold, unfeeling cement I lamented my life. I felt she had just about beat the will and intention to live out of me.

Basement Candy

Then, in an inexplicable yet warmly tangible moment, I felt a comforting presence, as if I was not alone. It was a welcome embrace, an approving nod, the kiss of one who loves you and a friendly face captured in the moment. This was the first time I felt the touchable, flesh-like presence of God. I knelt in awe and sudden peace, knowing in an instant that I could sustain life—with God's presence within. I wanted to package up those feelings and tuck them in my pocket so I could take them out and peek at them on hard days. But the feelings themselves dissipated like the fog in the fall when the sun arrives. However, the knowing that I had just encountered the God of my prayers lingered. Even as I write I am reliving that moment and chills run up my spine, reminders of the visceral presence of that intrigue.

Now, I barely remember life before the hospital. I am still sad, many of my relationships feel hollow, I spend most of my time by myself, and my personhood has been stripped of all the trappings that used to make it seem festive—accomplishments, jobs, accolades, crowds, influence, etc. The unveiling of my emotions has exposed the raw nerves of depression and anxiety. Now those emotions roll in and out like the ocean at high tide.

My emotions are held together by pharmaceuticals, two to four appointments a week with doctors and therapists, spilled coffee, stubbornness, and prayer. To make this a weightier matter, the drugs have contributed to a seventy-pound gain, mostly in my ass. I am basically a yellow, round, sad-faced emoji in yoga pants.

Ironically, it wasn't until they began to treat the symptoms of my complex-PTSD that I discovered I have social anxiety. As some of the more affective symptoms, such as depression and dissociation, began to come under control, other symptoms became clearer. One of those was the people anxiety.

When I am in stores my stomach churns and becomes so upset that I seldom make it through one stop without visiting a restroom. When I am in a group setting, the same thing happens, and often I become so exhausted from managing my emotions and symptoms that I am worn out for the rest of the day and sometimes for days to follow. This includes social gatherings, church, and concerts or events for my children.

Traveling can be especially problematic as airports, trains, and buses are filled with noise and unanticipated interaction, and restrooms can be hard to find. I take medication to pretreat my stomach and nerves before I travel.

I am often frustrated by all these accommodations and long to be like "normal people" while in public. But being open about my life has given me new perspective on how to live well within my capabilities. I now know that I'm not alone and maybe not even as weird as I think I am. Sharing my life with others has given me the freedom to be myself, even in a public space.

Society has taught us to go hard at everything without recognizing the cost of living a life of imbalance. Balance is an elusive concept. We tend to work and play with abandon. I can stress myself out and expend all my energy but if I don't replenish or recharge myself I'm left exhausted and depleted. I have the freedom to use all my time giving to others but if I forget to express generosity and care to myself my mental health and emotional health suffers.

I once heard someone say that self-care is not a biblical concept, which I respectfully disagree with. Caring for ourselves mentally, spiritually, and physically is crucial to our experience as believers. Scripture is replete with examples of heroes of faith, even Jesus himself, taking time to pray, meditate, eat, and rest. My ability to care for and maintain this flawed, earthly body I have been gifted with is directly related to honoring Christ.

There are seasons in life where we are called on to give sacrificially to those around us but in order to retain a sustainable life of worship we need to balance those times with active and intentional care of self. In my opinion this isn't about living life selfishly but about living life wisely, using the resources available to us.

14

Canned Promises

SLOWING DOWN TO BE present at the hospital was difficult. I wasn't good at slowing down. Ever since childhood I had been busy. My busyness kept the emotional pain of a tragic childhood from me. If I was busy I didn't have time to consider myself. In high school my science teacher told me "Jill, you don't burn the candle at both ends. You break it in half and burn all four." I always kept busy so as to not disturb Marilyn or anger her. I practiced piano for hours a day because I was competing and played for all the high school choirs and the church orchestra. I was the choir president, very active in the church youth group, and led the high school on-campus Bible study. I was exhausted even then.

My adulthood was a blur of activity and responsibility. We had four children in five and a half years. Between children and work schedules it was a crazy time of life but I loved being a mommy. Precious memories of their soft little heads and chubby bodies warm my heart.

During the years when I was working on starting a church I worked until my chest hurt so bad I would curl up on my office floor until the burn subsided. I was late to everything and rushed through every conversation and event like a race horse with blinders on. Just get through it. Don't stop. Don't get sidetracked. Just run.

But then I couldn't outrun the past anymore. My brain and nervous system wouldn't allow it. I was arrested by crippling emotional pain and fatigue.

Post-Traumatic Faith

The serene grounds of the hospital and uncomplicated life, with meals and cleaning all provided, was miles away from my busy world. However, having these things provided allowed me to focus on myself, which was uncomfortable and messy, but necessary. I was cocooned by the system.

Growing up we were poor. Marilyn refused to accept government help, in spite of the fact that she was a single mother with an eighth grade education trying to raise three kids. She was proud and stubborn. Nobody was going to tell her what to do or how to do it.

One of my least favorite things about being poor was sharing bathwater. Mom would run a bath. Park got the first dip, since he was the oldest, then Dana', and finally me. She would run a little hot water into the cold water for me to warm it up a bit. Filthy scum floated and bathtub rings formed from the Ivory soap.

Food was a precious commodity. I know what it is like to see empty cupboard shelves, empty freezers, and empty refrigerators. When there was food, I never saw name brands in our cupboards or sugar cereals on the shelf. The only exception was when we were sick, Marilyn would take us to the store to pick out a box of whatever kind of cold cereal we wanted as a comfort treat. I choked down Captain Crunch and Strawberry Shortcake with the sharp blade-like pain of tonsillitis, just for the joy of having that treat. Some Sunday nights we had fried potatoes for dinner. It was really special if there was cheddar cheese to put on top of our skillet-seared salty potatoes. I remember the powdered milk where she wrote neatly on the box top exactly how many glasses she would get out of one box if we had our one glass a day. We had one small half glass of juice in the morning with our Flintstones chewable vitamins and bland generic cereal. There was also a phase where she would mix wheat germ or barley or some other such nonsense into the juice, rendering it terrible but supposedly healthy. I went to friends' houses where they didn't have restrictions on how much milk or juice they drank. It seemed unfathomable that such a world existed.

Many warm summer days in the 1980s found us following behind the machines in the Spokane valley, picking through clods of dirt and greenery to discover the green beans, cucumbers, and strawberries that were too small for the machines to pick. I hated those hot, dirty fields where sweat pooled on your back and the sun burned your arms, but participation was not optional. This food was necessary for our sustenance.

We had a friend who used to go through grocery store dumpsters and pick out the produce that had been thrown out. He would pile the flat bed trailer up with the imperfect, spoiled food and bring it to our house. When the half-rotted food arrived, a flurry of activity followed. Because the food had already started decomposing, we were in a race against time to clean and preserve it. We sat on the brick red octagon bench around the backyard oak tree and worked feverishly. We cut the "bad" parts of the fruit off. The rotted, brown, mushy worm-eaten parts were discarded. I hated the thought of eating food pre-sampled by slimy worms. Nevertheless, we snapped beans, cleaned peaches, scrubbed berries, and sliced cucumbers with a frenzy.

Then we cleaned it and began preserving. Canning. A tedious, lengthy process of boiling, seasoning, and sealing all of those hot mason jars to preserve the salvaged goodness. I spent many hours in the kitchen, sitting on a tall wooden stool at the long yellow table, counting the "pop" of the jar lids to make sure each one sealed properly.

In our rustic cement basement that smelled of stale smoke from the wood stove and crawl space dirt, I loved to look at the colorful jars of produce on the shelves. As much as I hated the work that brought the food, the colorful, perfectly lined-up jars were beautiful. I'll be the first to admit that nothing beats homemade pickles, applesauce, peaches, strawberry jam, etc.

Though canning was plentiful, hunger wasn't unfamiliar. One day I'd had enough. I had that gnawing, achy hunger that makes one feel as if they are going to go crazy if they don't satiate it. There would be no food until dinner and we didn't snack because we didn't have extra food for such frivolities. However, on this day I knew there were peanuts in the cabinet. The good kind, in the curved bottle with the blue and yellow label. Roasted. Delicious. I decided a teeny handful would satisfy the deep rumblings of my belly. I ate them. They didn't absolve my hunger but they did give me courage that I could survive until dinner.

Unbeknownst to me, Mom had drawn a line on the jar in black sharpie marker indicating the level of nuts in the jar. My small handful of contraband had dropped the peanuts below that line.

She beat me that day with a big stick. As I stretched out over that patchwork quilt on the bed, waiting for her to hit me, in spite of my fear, the only thought I had was that I was so hungry.

First she hit my butt with that big board, wielding her anger and bitterness with power. My body reacted to the white hot explosion of pain. It reverberated through my system. To make it worse, when she hit us we were not allowed to cry out or respond. She would taunt me, "What's wrong?

Why are you crying:?" She wanted silence, which is impossible to achieve when a body is under that kind of duress. She beat me not as discipline but from a place deep inside of her that was angry, bitter, and hungry for revenge of some sort. She beat me viciously until welts appeared and bruises started to form on my butt, legs, and back. I didn't get dinner.

15

Dirty Laundry

All day, everyday, depression lies like a heavy, inviting, itchy, smelly blanket. You may want to leave that smelly cocoon but it is too damn heavy to move by yourself. At the same time, you want to stay in your blanket cave. You are fully aware that it's a cold world out there and so shedding the blanket sounds stupid. This is depression.

Recently, I woke up early. I was really disappointed about that, not because I needed extra sleep but because I hadn't yet formed my brain into something to look forward to. I used to wake up with a laundry list of tasks begging for my attention. The point is, even if I feel purposeless, the tasks at hand, my drive to succeed and/or my sense of over responsibility would usually drag me through the day until I found something that felt a lot like meaning to hang on to.

Now I have no schedule or calendar to march me through the day. Instead I have a smorgasbord, a veritable feast of time laid out in front of me with all sorts of delicious possibilities. Only I'm not hungry. Why force myself to participate or choose from that buffet when there is no internal motivation? It is a weird sort of black hole to fall into where nobody has any expectations on your daily life. It is there you begin to realize how much our lives revolve around the expectation of others. At one time I had no time to even catch my breath. Now I have the advantage of all the time in the world. Sadly, it's all Monopoly money, useless to spend and meaningless to even try.

Post-Traumatic Faith

I don't like change but resisting it appears to make little difference. I didn't imagine this is what my life would be in my mid-forties but with a little strength, active faith, and a modicum of patience I am hoping I will make it through.

The secrecy and silence that Marilyn instilled in us about our abuse is legendary. As a little girl, I stared myself down in the mirror, willing myself not to cry, be angry, or show any emotion. Emotions were fodder for her to pounce on weaknesses, to exploit for her own emotional outlet. I shuttered my mind, steeling myself to disappear to a place where her words, blows, and silences couldn't hurt me.

1980, eight years old. I strained to see over my shoulders in the mirror, twisting to get a good angle to look at my back. I was not admiring the white eyelet shirt I was wearing. I was making sure there was no blood seeping through the fabric. Marilyn had beat me again. This time across the back with a switch, leaving stripes, cuts, and open sores. As always, I was convinced I did something to deserve the whipping. In my mind the shame was mine to carry, so I held it, tucking it in like a secret under my shirt with the welts.

The consequences of letting people know our "family secrets," or as she called it "airing our dirty laundry," were dire. She claimed the youth pastor told her what we talked and prayed about. Supposedly our friends' parents told her what we chatted about to our friends. According to her, our teachers also told her about all our behavior and conversations at school. We were convinced that the whole world was reporting on us on the regular. Besides, she told us everybody was on her side. Why would I doubt her?

My sister shared with me that we once told a church friend's mother what was happening in the house. That mother called Marilyn to tell her what we were saying. We received such horrible beatings that I don't even remember the incident. I only know of it because my sister told me. So we hid everything and kept our suffering to ourselves. One year my sister, a teenager, wore long pants and turtlenecks for an entire summer to cover the open wounds on her back and legs. Nobody inquired as to why.

In 1989, during the fall of my senior year of high school, Marilyn sat down at the dining room table with me. She very matter-of-factly said, "I can discipline you however I want to. I am your God given authority and I can kill you if I have to." I couldn't believe those words would ever come out of her mouth, but it was especially surreal since the conversation wasn't spoken in the middle of an argument. I had not provoked her. It was simply a cold, premeditated, calculated statement, meant to terrify me. Which it did.

The following February 1990, on a Friday, I told Mr. Carlson, a science teacher whom I trusted completely, that if I didn't come back to school on Monday, he should come look for me. Years later I found out this conversation triggered a Department of Family Services (DFS) intervention. Mrs. Stransky, my school counselor, was also involved. It was too little too late, but in retrospect I appreciate their advocacy.

My beloved choir teacher, Mrs. Terhark, took me out for a ride one February afternoon, under the pretense that we were picking out costumes for next year's choirs. As we drove around the beautiful lake, she asked me, "Are you in danger? Does she hit you?" I answered "Yes" to both questions. "Do you have any place to go?" she asked. "Yes," I said. My friend, Shari, knew I was struggling and had asked her parents if I could stay with them. They said "anytime" and I knew this was my out. "You need to go home right now, pack your things while your mother is at work, and leave," she instructed.

I did as I was instructed. I put all my things in white garbage bags. I remembered to grab the card file Marilyn kept on all my friends and the phone book where she had highlighted everybody we knew, in an effort to keep my location secret. I called my friend and asked her to come get me. We threw everything in her red Geo Metro and drove away.

All I could tell Shari's parents was that I was depressed. I didn't even remember the incidents of abuse that happened that fall or winter. I couldn't express the abuse because I was systematically erasing it from my mind by dissociating from the present. I was numb but functioning. I was afraid to go to school because I was sure Marilyn was going to show up and kill me.

Shari's mom, Sharon, called Dana' and told her I was with them. Dana' began to tell her stories of the abuse. A couple of days after I moved in, Sharon and her husband, Jim, explained to me that in order to protect me, we needed to go to the Department of Family Services (DFS) and talk to them, since Marilyn had listed me as a runaway. The police were actively looking for me. Sharon and I went to DFS together. She recounted her conversation with Dana' to the DFS officer.

Now, four years after Sandy and Marilyn divorced, when DFS sought to take custody of me, they got in touch with Sandy. He showed up and testified to that horrible beating, affirming my accusations of mistreatment at the hand of Marilyn. I don't know why he waited so long to act on my behalf but it meant the world to me that he contributed at that crucial moment. He was the only insider who could/would talk about what happened in our house and testify to her treatment.

The police explained to me that they needed to inform Marilyn that I had been found and they needed her to sign off parental custody to the state. We all had to go meet with her. As we left the DFS office, the child specialist assigned to me gave me some instructions. "We know that a single look, movement, or word can be threatening. When we meet your mother, if she scares you, then you can get up and walk out and we will all follow you. We are there for you!" I didn't believe her.

On the way to the house the police officer I was riding with, Jerry, asked me, "Do you have anything against police officers?" I didn't think it wise to tell him I was terrified of them, so I said nothing. "I have a friend who is a police officer and they are foster parents. I think you would do great with them." This seemed like a very bad idea but I didn't have enough agency to be able to speak my own mind, so I kept silent.

Jerry asked me what I wanted to do after I graduated. On that very scary night, feeling like all the anxiety in the world coursing through my body, I told Jerry I wanted to be a pastor and that I was going to attend Bible college. He told me his family were Christian missionaries. It was comforting conversation in the midst of the turmoil.

Once at the house, Marilyn and her best friend were waiting for us in the living room. It was quite an entourage; two officers, the child specialist, a child psychologist, and myself crammed into the living room of the little white house. The officers did what they promised. They got her to sign forms saying I had been found and that she was releasing custody to the state. After the business was done, Marilyn said, "I want to talk to Jill alone. You guys can just stand outside, on the other side of the glass door, on the covered front porch." I didn't know what she wanted to say. I just knew that I didn't want to hear it. I rose from the couch, walked out the door, and I'll be damned if the whole team didn't get up and walk out after me, leaving the two of them stunned.

After we left, Jerry told me that I would be staying with his friends. To my tired and shocked mind it seemed as if we drove all around town before we ended up at the foster home. My foster parents, Tim and Debbie, greeted me at the door. My foster brother, a freshman, ran up the stairs and said "You're Jill Llafet! You run the Bible study at school that I have been looking for!" I think that immediately put his parents, who were previously only licensed to foster children age two and under, at ease. This ended up being an excellent, loving foster home where I felt safe and protected.

We waited a couple of months for the court case that would determine custody. On the appointed day, we entered the very austere, blond wood courtroom. Marilyn had chosen to represent herself. I had a public defender who was very kind and gracious. Marilyn was restless, fidgety, and out of control especially when I was on the stand. Several times when I was testifying she stood up and yelled, "She's lying." In absentia my sister had submitted a letter detailing the abuse and manipulation Marilyn put us through. On the other hand, my brother, also absent, wrote a glowing letter about what a model parent Marilyn had been. By then he had been gone long enough that he had blocked the violence and neglect out of his mind.

I had no support from the church. In fact, several ladies from the church testified under oath that Marilyn would never lay a hand on us, how she was an upstanding mother, and that we had been in their houses several times, without ever showing signs of abuse. All lies.

The state returned me to Marilyn's custody, citing the facts that I had no current marks on my body and that I was such a good student. "Every parent disciplines differently," the judge said dismissively. My public defender gave me his personal phone number. "That woman is going to kill you," he said. "You call me if you need me." The system failed me and the church failed me.

Marilyn had her best friend, Doris, tell me that I was to go live with her family for a while, so we could get things worked out. Three days later Doris told me that Marilyn had a nervous breakdown, didn't want anything to do with me and I could go anywhere I wanted to go. I just could not stay there. I went back to Shari's house where I stayed for the five months until I went to college. Marilyn and I exchanged fewer than ten words in next thirty-one years, until she died in 2020.

16

Moving On

WHEN THE TIME CAME to apply to college, Dana' sent me money for my application. Without Marilyn's knowledge, I applied for college in Missouri, which as previously stated, I hate. However, the school I was applying to seemed to have a superior program in the area of World Missions. However, after being abandoned by Marilyn in 1990 and left to make my own decisions, my thoughts began to change. All the sudden where I went to college was inconsequential as far as she was concerned. My need to run as far from her as money and opportunity allowed was gone. I began to look at the Pacific Northwest for a place that had a comparable program and found it at Northwest College in Kirkland, Washington, just east of Seattle.

I had scholarships and given the fact that I was an independent whom nobody could claim on taxes, lots of grant money. That, added to generous money from my guardian parents, allowed me, a poor student, to go to college. I also worked a lot. Too much, but I was always blessed with business jobs that paid the bills, along with ministry jobs that fed my soul.

My first college job was at a large law firm in nearby Bellevue. I cleaned coffee cups and made copies. Copious amounts of copies. One of my first tasks was copying an entire box of credit card receipts where a couple was going through and highlighting each and every thing they had purchased, dividing the debt down to the penny. Eventually, the firm put me on to answering the phones. I learned the phone system and taught myself to type on the typewriter that sat just to the right of the phone.

Moving On

Because the practice had a large family law section I was privy to a parade of broken families. Since Bellevue was one of the richest places in the nation at the time, thanks to Microsoft and Nintendo, there was a defined pattern to the divorces. A very rich man would come in, often with a tanned, manicured, beautiful, and much younger woman. His soon-to-be ex-wife would come in. Slightly overweight, emotional, and devastated, sometimes with teenage children in tow.

Soon I was moved into assisting paralegals in the office. I had my own desk and regular hours. Not bad for an eighteen-year-old. I worked in business law, and both ends of the life of money: probate and bankruptcy. Quickly, I became a student of how people arranged their money for postmortem use. I learned how quickly money could be made and lost. And I filed so many letters of incorporation, business license renewals, and board of directors changes. It was a highly educational job which I loved.

During my freshman year of college my work as a pastor to the Korean students helped me begin to understand what a life of vocational ministry would be like and I loved it. I would take questions from what I learned in Bible 101 each week to my professor and then teach that lesson to the junior high, high school, and college students.

My sophomore year of college brought big changes also. That spring I was introduced to a pastor/attorney who was starting a church. He and two other men wanted me on the team. So I left the Korean community and together the four of us worked hard to establish a new community of faith, just north of the college. The church met in a junior high school. I taught the children in a locker room, stringing curtain rods across the bathroom doors, so I could use them as puppet theaters. The church grew, changed locations, grew some more, and eventually was blended into another congregation.

I have been told that there is one stage in your career that will never be matched by any other. It will always stand in your mind as the best of times. This team, Jim, Greg, and Don were my brothers, peers, pastors, friends. I loved them deeply. We worked together symbiotically, so much so that we made a pact that if one left, we all left. We either worked all together or separate. We had other staff and a string of interns, but we four stuck it out together. That experience, at nineteen years old, would never be matched by any other. It was a great five-year ride.

After my job at the law firm ended I switched jobs a couple of times before I got a job offer from a company that wanted me to do technical writing and graphics for them. They paid thousands of dollars to train me in graphics and then decided they wanted me in a different role. So, then they paid thousands to train me in project management software. I managed projects for 120 employees and 60 contractors. I made good money, which made up for the deficit of not being paid by the church. I was at the end of the church's shoestring budget and earned $50/month for my work. However, the graphics and project management training paid off immensely and were the starting points for a career in business consulting. The graphics knowledge came in handy with editing photos in my photography business.

I graduated with my undergraduate degree in 1994, but I didn't want to leave the academic world. I loved it. So, I entered graduate school at Seattle University. I worked early morning to mid-afternoon, drove into Seattle, took classes until seven in the evening and then went home. I studied spiritual formation, adult education, and curriculum. One of my goals was to be a college professor, instructing pastors on how to teach well.

17

Hallmark Holiday

Throughout adulthood I have applied every emotional avoidance tactic I can to Mother's Day. The memory of the moms I have lost overshadows the plastic joy of the hallmark holiday. Appreciation from my four beautiful children should satiate the longing I have for a mommy to call my own, but it doesn't.

I don't remember the mom who gave birth to me in Korea, in 1972. I've never had a burning desire to meet my biological mother. Maybe she loved me and circumstances beyond her control forced her to let go of me. Perhaps she just didn't want me. Her existence made my existence possible and for that I am grateful. However, that first breech of trust, letting me go, no matter the circumstances, doesn't ingratiate me to her.

In 1988, I watched the televised Olympic Games, hosted in Seoul. As the camera panned over the city, I burst into tears, understanding that somewhere in that vast, densely populated metropolis, somebody knew me. Somebody had my little face in their memory.

After I graduated from high school in 1990, Jay told me I was not adopted from Korea, but rather from inside the United States. I had belonged to another family in Detroit, who had adopted me but decided they couldn't keep me. I have no knowledge of why they chose to adopt me and then abandoned me. That mom stands as a sort of placeholder in time. The calendar says I was with her for a bit, but that is all I know. But knowing about her filled some questions I had about the adoption story I had been told.

Post-Traumatic Faith

Jay and Marilyn adopted me from that first set of American adopted parents, not from Korea. Marilyn always told me I flew straight from Korea, into Reno, on a big yellow airplane, and a nurse brought me out to their waiting arms. I always knew the story wasn't quite right. We used to get magazines from Holt adoption agency, through which the Park and Dana' were adopted. All the families had only two Korean adopted children because at that time that is all Korea would allow. However, there were three Korean children in my family—my older brother, Park, who is seven years older and my sister, Dana', who was four years older than I. None of us are blood siblings.

The big, yellow plane from Korea also puzzled me. As I got older, I knew Reno wasn't an international airport. No plane would have come there directly from Korea. It just didn't happen. And it seemed, from the Holt magazine, that everybody traveled to Korea to pick up their waiting child. Why didn't my parents do that for me?

Marilyn, who celebrated my arrival sometime before I turned two years old, is the mother that was the most formative. From her, I learned how to work hard. She was simply one of the hardest working people I have ever met.

We worked as a family to keep the lights on. We cleaned car dealerships after hours. My job was emptying cigarette butts from ashtrays, washing stale coffee from mugs, and emptying trash cans.

Together we shoveled out mobile homes after tenants left them disgusting and piled with trash. Marilyn worked in home health care and as a children's librarian. With the help of child support from Jay and a lot of elbow grease she was able to support the four of us. Not an easy accomplishment for someone with an eighth-grade education.

She fostered my creativity. One large drawer of an antique dresser in our living room was dedicated to my artistic pursuits. Humble supplies, paper, pencils, crayons, markers, and scissors were always at the ready. I often lay on the pea green, deep shag carpet, cutting, gluing, and coloring to my heart's content. I scoured every craft book in the library, finding things I could make for myself or gift to others. I built dollhouses out of shoe boxes and cut dozens of paper dolls out of magazines. Marilyn's old green cast-iron sewing machine, with its solid steel bobbins, was a beast to move but I sewed many happy hours on it. I made clothes for my dolls and King Louis, our black and white, extraordinarily docile cat. I made and dressed sock dolls, two of which sit in my craft room now.

I was a regular participant in the community classes that happened once a year around the local art festival "Art on the Green." The college green space, which is circumscribed by the big, beautiful lake, transformed itself into a huge outdoor art gallery. I took writing and newspaper/journalism classes. The big steamer trunk in our bedroom, that stands sentry around my memories, holds books and newspaper articles I authored as a grade school child during those summers.

From Marilyn, I learned to be passionate about learning. Many hot summer days found us riding our bikes, lugging backpacks filled with books back and forth to the library. We were academically advanced and, motivated by fear of her, did well in school. During fifth grade parent-teacher conferences in 1983, in Coeur d'Alene, Idaho, I remember sitting in our old brown and white Bronco outside of Sorenson Elementary. I was waiting in the car, which was steaming up in the sun and rain, praying there wouldn't be any hint of a bad teacher's report from my fifth grade teacher, Mr. McGinnis. If he had so much as breathed I wasn't compliant or that I was academically complacent, there would be hell to pay. I was sick with worry until she returned.

On the corner of our dining table sat the bible of table manners, *Miss Manners Basic Training: Eating*. We learned to have table manners fit for a queen. However torturous this was for us, this was a game for Marilyn. She loved to look up the proper ways to eat and behave at a table. Meals were taken with hair tied back, backs straight, shoes and shirts on. Please and thank you were mandatory. Loud chewing, slurping, and singing were verboten. We scooped soup in our bowls away from us instead of toward us, broke—never cut—rolls, never drank out of a bowl, and did not audibly scrape our plates. We were excused from the table formally.

Unfortunately, from Marilyn I also took in first-hand knowledge of fear, pain, rejection, humiliation, and how to keep secrets. Because of her, or rather the fear of her, I learned to mask my emotions and my scars and with every day that passes I learn about loss. To absorb the loss of the mother who chose me but then didn't want me is soul numbing.

There are more mothers. There is a guardian mother who protected me at my most vulnerable and kept me safe until I could enter the adult world. She loves her children and mine fiercely. The safe and kind foster mother who agreed to take me, a seventeen-year-old runaway, even though she was only licensed to care for children under the age of two. Rounding out the set is the mother-in-law who we had the privilege of making a Nana first. The sad fact is, I have many moms, but I don't have enough of them to fill the chasm the loss of a mom created. I just wanted the mom who would tuck me in at night.

To advocate keeping children with their parents, when safe and possible, is to do the work of the Holy. A heart can only be spliced so many ways and mine felt like it was shattered. As I grew into adulthood, I feared that I had so little heart left that it would never be big enough to hold a family of my own.

I was bullied through childhood and into adulthood. My childhood was filled with fear and angst. Being raised this way taught me a lot of things about parenting. In addition to hoping our children would be people of wisdom, character, and great faith, I have lived with some internal, seldom spoken goals for them.

I only heard my Marilyn say she was sorry one time. Because of this, I want my children to hear "I'm sorry." I'm not particularly good at this, but I try. As a parent, I found it is difficult to submit yourself to the inevitability that we can be wrong. However, I am convinced that while our mistakes may be epic, our ability to ask for forgiveness is redeeming.

When our first baby was eighteen months old I panicked. I had read somewhere, no doubt in my college textbooks, that everything a child needs to be healthy and thrive is established before they turn eighteen months old. I wondered if I had done enough. Had I given her the foundation she needed? I had no idea what I was doing so what if I hadn't prepared this precious, chubby baby for a healthy emotional future? That feeling would dissipate but gurgled up again with each child.

I do love being a mom. People ask me frequently if it was chaos with so many little kids at once. I don't remember it being crazy, just busy. The only time it felt crazy was when Brittany was sick with leukemia at two years old. At that time I consistently felt like I was hanging on by my fingernails.

But the kids bring me joy, make me so very proud, and honor me well with their lives and their words. I draw deep satisfaction from watching them grow and mature.

I am a mom but I'm not that mom. You know, the one who does everything correct and with a flourish and extra dab of whipped cream? I wish I were. If I were that mom I would have made my children breakfast, lunch, *and* dinner. I would have done their laundry and been gracious about taking things to the school when they forgot them at home. If I were that mom I would have stayed up late with them while they finished homework and maybe even helped them with it. That mom would have attended and enjoyed all of their activities (even junior high school band and choir), sitting in the front row with a camera at every one of them. But I'm not.

I'm the other kind of mom. I'm the mom who numbered the children, which seemed easier than trying to remember their names. I'm the mom who hardly ever remembered their friend's names. And Lord help me if my kids ever needed their social security number. I'm the mom who told my children the ice cream truck was a music truck so they wouldn't ask for ice cream every time it came around. I'm the mom who taught my children to do laundry and gave them assigned days to do it so I wouldn't have to. I'm the mom who ate their treats out of their stockings and Easter baskets. I'm the mom who loved to work and sometimes forgot to take care of my household because I was too engrossed.

But I'm also the mom who loved to let the kids bring as many people home as possible to eat all my food. I'm the mom who let the children all pile on top of me, which they saw as an act of love and not aggression. I'm the mom who said I needed to run errands and hid at Target for an hour. I'm the mom who was good at providing activities for the kids to do but wasn't so good at playing with them. I'm the mom who enjoyed hosting the kids at our fire pit, so they could talk and listen to music, and sing on the patio below my bedroom window.

No matter what kind of mom I am, there is always somebody to compare with who seemed to do the job better than I did. But I did my best. No matter what, I'm the mom God gave to these children and they love me. And I love them, even though I forget their names.

As a parent my goal was that my children would have joyful, happy memories of their childhood. I believe kids should enjoy being kids. They should have dirt on their faces, Play-Doh under their fingernails, and endless bicycle adventures. Their mental scrapbook should have wonderful memories bursting off the pages.

We enjoyed our teenagers. I loved their laughter and their groups of friends who ate freely from our refrigerator. Their game nights were loud, raucous, and crazy. My happiest times were when they had their friends packed into our little house, enjoying one another. They were one huge, noisy amoeba, eating and drinking everything in its wake. I loved them. They were happy. I loved that they loved being in our house and enjoyed themselves here. Their laughter is sunshine.

As they have turned into young adults, we are proud of them and enjoy seeing them reach dreams and become great people. These children of ours have turned into some great adults.

When I was a teenager I was not happy. Nobody wanted to come hang out at our house. It was intimidating and wrought with expectation of proper behavior. Marilyn wanted to be the center of every conversation, sitting on the couch in the middle of our conversation, while adjusting the coffee table books and magazines to exacting distance from one another.

While I was always afraid of Marilyn, convinced my next mistake would lead to a beating or other severe consequences, I didn't want my children to live in fear. I believed that our children needed healthy respect and good boundaries and I didn't want them to live afraid. I wanted them to enjoy lives and be enjoyed by those around them.

My trauma therapists and doctors repeatedly tell me that I obviously learned somewhere in my early life how to love—because I am capable of giving and receiving love, which can be unlikely as a child of abuse. I had every set up for not being able to bond with people, to be able to give or receive love because of attachment issues. Yet I have a beautiful, healthy, and very loud family of my own. I made a lot of mistakes along the way but our family thrived. Why? Because I had excellent modeling by good people in my life, despite the bad ones who raised me. Because I had the grounding of the church and my faith in God, which gave me direction and a road map to follow. Because I was determined to be what my parents were not.

Marilyn,

My children are the most amazing, precious gift. They live life vibrantly. I am so proud of all they are and love having a front row seat to their future.

To think every mother feels this way would be foolish. However I would hope every child would feel at least love and compassion from their parent. But not you. You couldn't even manage the most basic of human kindness or emotion for your children.

It is stunning to me how you could mangle the bodies, relationships, and futures of three children that you took such effort to get? We were not an accident. We were actually part of a plan. And we were no less beautiful or deserving of love than my four kids are. You squandered your opportunity for love, threw away a chance at the family you craved, by letting the demons and errors of your past overwhelm the strongest power of the universe, a mother's love. You became an evil, twisted version of your upbringing and took abuse

Hallmark Holiday

and evil to sickening new heights. Your words destroyed our hearts, your spirituality sucked our souls, your hatred poisoned our minds, and your blows confirmed your self-hatred and a disregard for life.

I remember your face as you beat me. Not angry, sad, or remorseful. Your face was calm and relaxed as you wielded 2 x 4s, hangers, extension cords, butter churns, branches, belts, and hatred. I shudder at the realization that every time I looked at an object near you I made estimates as to whether you would use it as a weapon. Mentally, I considered how that stool, that chair, that ladder would feel if it crashed into me. Too often I got to find out.

Over the years I have spent hours trying to figure out why you would beat me until blood ran down my back, and leave bruises and cuts that took weeks to heal. Finally, I gave up. The fact is, there is no logical answer and no compassionate reasoning that can justify the crimes you committed against us.

You were a horrid example of a Christ follower and almost polluted my entire view of the God of the Bible. I appreciate that you put me in a position to meet my Jesus, the only place where I have consistently felt safe and loved. While I am confused as to the "master plan" of my being given to your care, I am singularly grateful for the grace, hope, and love I find in God.

Now, I know. I deserved better. The best even. Not because I earned or deserved it for being extra special. Just because I was a beautiful, innocent child. I did not deserve you!

So, I could not fight back then and I will not now. I will, however, go on about my life. I will enjoy the love of my family because I chose not to repeat the sick pattern of abuse. I will be celebrated by myself and by countless friends and family. I will not look over my shoulder and see the smoke from all the relational bridges I burned. Most of all I will live at peace—an emotion and joy you could not imagine. I will not live with regret for not making amends because of my stubbornness and I will not let my past mistakes consume my tomorrows.

In spite of you, I can and will live and thrive. You threatened to take my life but you failed. So I will walk out my days confident that I was meant to live and thrive. The childhood you robbed from me will not control my future. I will live joyfully.

Jill 10/19/2015

18

Technicolor

To Brittany from Mommy: January 2001

I will forever remember January 24, 2001. On that day, the earth seemed to shudder to a stop and then change course, forever. My world will never be the same again. Ever since you started to show personality you showed an incredible, loving, gentle spirit. I know every mother thinks this of her child, but you are truly special. You love everybody and they in turn open their arms to you. You are an angel wrapped in a chubby, happy face.

I had even dared to think that perhaps you were one of those children that God lends for a while to us, to brighten the world and then takes to keep for Himself. I rue the day those thoughts crossed my mind because now I am scared they may come true.

On January 24, after a doctor's appointment to determine the cause of your high fever and finding no cause, they requested we have blood work done on you. Through a rapid course of events they diagnose you with leukemia. Cancer. One of the scariest words known to man (and mom) suddenly becomes a familiar resident in our minds and mouths. You are very ill and your body is close to shutting down.

How is it possible for a child to be this ill, I wonder? This happens to the people that live in magazines. This most certainly does not happen to my children. Perhaps there has been a mistake? Days *pass. More tests. In the end they determine that you definitely have cancer. The unthinkable becomes reality.*

In your hospital room there is a list of medicines that would be used in the event you need to be resuscitated. For the first time it hits me. I may lose you! How would I live and breathe. I can't even think through that. Not because I deny it could happen but because it hurts so much to admit it.

How did this happen to you? Now you are not strong and lively and silly. Now you are vulnerable, weak, and fragile. Now I do not push you to play and explore, to be brave and adventurous. Now my heart holds you and protects you from all the elements in this world that can harm you. Sadly, the greatest enemy we fight lives deep within your bones and blood, out of reach of my protective arms.

THE TERROR THAT IS cancer touched our world when our toddler was diagnosed with leukemia. In the course of two hours we went from what we thought was a child with an ear infection to a child with cancer. One doctor's visit and a blood draw. That's all it took to turn our lives upside down. I remember driving home from the hospital to pack for our emergency trip to Denver, Colorado, the closest children's hospital, and thinking about who would officiate her funeral. We had no way of knowing the severity or even the treatment plan for her. I had no idea whether chemo was a light ray, pill, liquid, or some voodoo telepathic medicine. We were foreigners in this new-to-us land of cancer. All we knew was that her life was in immediate danger and we needed to go to Denver ASAP.

When the doctors first told us they were going to put in a mediport to administer her medicines, steroids, and chemo, I felt nauseous. I wanted to tell them no, they couldn't cut my child open, but they weren't really asking. That port made giving her necessary treatment so much easier on her.

In Denver, as we walked through the blood and heart ward to access the cancer ward, we saw children who were deformed and struggling to stay alive. Then we would leave that ward and approach rooms with a radioactive symbol on the door. Before that the only thing I had seen a radioactive symbol on was a bomb. And now my child was behind those doors.

To walk through an entire hallway of kids held prisoners by their disease was overwhelming to my senses. I have found no place more difficult to see the goodness of God than in a hospital ward for children with catastrophic and chronic diseases. And yet I also saw the face of God, in the faces of the doctors who cared for us, the nurses who tirelessly lifted the spirits of children and families all day long. I could see the image of God in the faces of children who were suffering and yet enduring. Brittany's room was the last one on the hall before the transplant wing of the cancer treatment center. Every day we would watch the traffic through those doors and marvel at the medicine that had been created to save the lives of countless children.

Taryn was four months old, Brittany two, Alexander four, and Emily almost six when Brittany was diagnosed. Kids with cancer are amazing, as are their siblings. Overall, the less jumpy and reactive we were, the more normative treatment became. Once acclimated to the environment of treatment, which I highly recommend parents induct the whole family into, kids generally befriend their environment. We hauled the kids to most doctor's appointments, where they got special attention as part of a weird little family of cancer patients and families. We tried hard to find the joy and fun in our surroundings, however difficult that was.

During long stays at the hospital in Billings, the nurses held tea parties and let the kids "help" at the information desk. We watched the Disney Christmas story hundreds of times and ate more Cheetos and grilled cheese than a body should in their entire lifetime. The baby napped in the playroom wagon and all five of us took siesta every day together.

Three years of treatment and dozens of hospital stays later, she was done with treatment. The mediport I initially resisted became a security blanket I wanted to hang on to. I didn't want it taken out in case it was what saved her life! But it had outlived its usefulness, so they took it out.

I cannot adequately sum up the toll those three years took on us, except to say that it is a blur.

My anxiety peaked during that time. I used to stand at the kitchen sink doing dishes and cry because my hands hurt so bad. The skin would flake and peel from the cuticles down my fingers, flake off my palms and bleed. I lost weight, I couldn't sleep, and was so tired all the time. Nobody told me that I could take something to help with the anxiety—I don't know that I even had language to describe what I was feeling at that time. I only knew to take it one day at a time, pulling, fighting as hard as I could against the deep feelings of despair.

At the end of her treatment I fell into a deep depression. I quit eating almost entirely and lost thirty pounds in two months. I was overwhelmed by everything, which didn't make sense because I had just survived my child's cancer! I didn't know what I was experiencing until a doctor finally told me I had depression. I just thought I was exhausted and couldn't pull myself through another joyless day.

Technicolor

It was the first time anybody had told me I was depressed and put me on medication. Six weeks after starting medication I was sitting in a meeting with four other pastors. All of a sudden it was as if somebody had turned the lights on or we had reached the end of the black and white part of *The Wizard of Oz*. Technicolor waves lifted the fog from my brain and I felt like myself again. All of the sudden I could feel the difference between the dark and the light.

Depression. Anxiety. These are almost socially acceptable maladies. While not as common as the cold, or as publicized as cancer, they are at least within grasp of understanding. We no longer have to gate check these illnesses when we enter into personal conversation. However, we start to get a little air-sick when talking about more extreme mental illness. And we certainly are not progressive enough to converse about seriously heavy baggage like suicidal ideation or homicidal intent.

It's been eight years since I was hospitalized. I would like to say that I'm healed. I'm back better than ever. But mental illness doesn't work that way. Sometimes it's more like a blister; you know the irritant is there but you don't quite expect it to fester so much. During the day, I can be found breathing shallower, quicker. I glance at my hands on the steering wheel and observe they are fidgety or gripping the steering wheel tightly. I'm a little more irritable than usual at the slow traffic, slow kids, and dumb dog.

And then it happens. All of a sudden, I'm in a full-blown anxious state. My brain is racing, I suddenly have no space, time, energy, or money to complete anything, and the world is going to explode at any minute. Everything is happening at once and I am powerless to stop it. Everything is bad. Nothing is good. And usually, I'm the cause of it all going to hell. I have increasingly less anxious and depressed days than I used to, but they still exist. They remind me to keep up with treatment, meds, and self care. I try. I fail and I try again.

Every year since my kids were little, I have added a Christmas book to our collection that comes out at the same time as the tree. One of my favorites contains photographs of single snowflakes. Photographers have captured snowflakes and photographed them in proper lighting before they melt. The images are intricate, glorious, and wholly unique.

I would like to hold my moments—the beautiful, the depressed, the anxious, and the misinformed ones—inspect them up against the light, and let them melt away peacefully like the snowflakes, without any anxiety or wish for them to last longer.

19

When Churches Are Assholes

I LOVED SERVING IN the church. I love the church, for what it can be when at its best. I loved seeing what it could be in the darkest hours and how it can resuscitate and redefine itself. In its buildings I find a familiarity and a peace that I find nowhere else. It's the peace of sitting by the ocean listening to the waves. It is the joy of sitting among books in a beautiful library, curled up among the gabled ceilings. It is the wonderful smell of a freshly washed baby. Unexpected and delightful hope.

I can sit at its worn altars and pray to a God I am confident hears me. I sit with my Bible open. The passage I am reading is the affirmation I need from God, a suggested readjustment of my attitude or a recalibrating of my spiritual journey. It is real and tangible to me, like a letter from a friend. It's personal and global all at the same time.

I am a woman. I am a mom, a wife, a pastor, a daughter, a businesswoman, and a friend. I wear many hats and am defined by many titles and yet, I am always Jill, no matter the moniker used to describe me. Similarly, the church is a building. It is a group of people. It is an institution and an eclectic stamp collection of loosely connected, mismatched religious beliefs. All under one name—the church. As I reflect on my time with the church, the institution, I realize that it's the people I truly love, not the institution.

I most often think of the church as a body of people. And I think of Jesus. Not white Jesus that hung over our piano in his golden frame, with perfect countenance, glowing skin, serene. The Middle Eastern, scrappy, loving, holy man who lived a life of love. His love was not always pretty, but it was always perfect, timely, and right. This is the hope and focus of the church I love.

This is how I was able to quarantine the hurt people of the church caused me and continue to work inside the institution, without bitterness toward the whole. From a young age I knew the church was flawed because it was made up of people. People possess the ability to be both good and evil, light and dark. The church, when it's on its best behavior, possesses the ability to affect the world in good, benevolent, and gracious ways. I have loved the church for the potential of what it could do for the world. I believed in what I peddled with my whole heart.

However, the institution can be an asshole. There is an underbelly of the church that is pockmarked with warts, scars, festering sores, and self-inflicted wounds. When an individual hurts another person it can be catastrophic. When a church, intentionally or by negligence, gets it wrong, the fallout is nuclear. When a place that is supposed to be the epicenter and example of love harms people, it creates distrust and cataclysmic damage to the image and soul purpose of the institution. And paramount in the church's mission is taking primary responsibility for the safety of its children. I experienced the neglect and abandonment of the church firsthand.

When I was eight years old, while at our private Christian school/church, my mother, who was working as the school secretary, was angry at me for something. She pulled me out of class and instructed me to get a switch from a tree in the yard. I brought it into the school. She stripped me and beat me in that church bathroom until welts covered my body. We were within clear earshot of the classrooms but nobody stopped her. Nobody came to my rescue. Corporal punishment was sanctioned by the church, and parental authority had the final word.

When I was in junior high I heard a minister preach about his "call" to the clergy. He said his father used to beat his mother terribly. He and his six siblings were beat until they bled. However, by the preacher's testimony, God promised his mother that if she stayed with her husband, all the children would be in the ministry. As a child of abuse, sitting and listening to the purposeful usage of God as a conduit of harm to children, I was outraged. Confused. Angry. Why would God *tell* a mother that she could allow irreparable harm to her children, just so they could have occupation within the church? What a terrible price to pay.

Post-Traumatic Faith

I became a pastor in spite of my abuse, but I carry emotional and mental wounds that, under pressure, burst open in my mid-forties. Each encounter with crisis has the potential to open one of those wounds, and if not treated, it either festers or explodes without any apparent provocation.

At Navigate, the church I had started in 2009, I had a man who worked with sex offenders ask if the men he worked with could come to the church. It created an ethical, moral, and spiritual dilemma for me. I want everybody to have a place of worship. However, while people are in the church building, I was ultimately responsible for their well-being. Could I make a safe place for all? There were children in my building that, while they were there, I was bound to protect. Eventually, the men decided to hold a Bible study at the house instead of attending a church gathering, but I know I would have erred on the side of protecting the children. That was my job.

At another church I caught wind that a junior high young man had been found in the school's girls bathroom exposing himself. The investigation as to whether there had been additional abuse was ongoing. The pastor I worked for at the time did not want me to ask the mom to keep the boy, who was prone to wander, close during services. I wanted to have a conversation with the single mom and her son about how we could best keep everybody safe and protected. What I intended as a conversation was perceived as a threat and aggression toward the family so I backed up. I did not, however, let the matter go. I was determined to keep our children safe. So, every Sunday as soon as he entered the building there were seven men at the ready. At all times, whenever Derek was on campus, somebody had eyes on him. This was for his security, not wanting him to endure any false accusations and for the safety of the church body.

Defending the young and weakest among us is priority to our faith. Conversely, not defending those in our care can be catastrophic and cause trauma. Our priorities, at the behest of Jesus, are to care for the weak, widowed, abandoned, and fatherless. To be the church is to take this call seriously.

In 1990, my last semester of my senior year of high school, as the noose of secrecy and abuse began to squeeze the life out of me, I started reaching out to teachers and pastors for help. My youth pastor got the school to release me one day for an hour. He and his wife took me to Dairy Queen. As we sat with our mid-day treat, he asked me, "Does she ever hit you?" I lied and told them "no." I sensed he already knew the answer was "yes," but they accepted my answer and returned me to school. I later found out that upon introducing my plight to the pastoral staff of the church, he was instructed to not get involved. It was a "domestic matter" and the church was not to be a part of it. Tell me. If the church doesn't get involved in domestic matters that involve the harm of the child then what good is it? What purpose does it serve, if not for that?

Despite this betrayal, somehow, I decided that the church was made up of people, who could be mean, angry, hurtful, and flat-out dumpster fires. But I believed that God was good, despite people's attempt to twist and mangle his message of love. A smidgen of hope was preserved in me that God would help.

When a place of worship, a literal sanctuary and school for the soul, abandons its congregants while in their hour of need, it proves itself irrelevant. So, given the circumstances, why would I follow a path that led me straight into the church rather than away from it? It's because I believed in her. No matter the behavior of some people in the church, I just believed it could be better. My faith in God outweighed my disappointment in people. Not to say that I wasn't ever disappointed in God. I was. I was bitterly disappointed that he didn't allow me to escape Marilyn or Jay. With tears in my eyes and a tortured body, I wondered why God would allow these things to happen to me, one whom he loves. There are no answers, only unrequited questions.

We, the people of the church, can love, serve, and be better. My frustration is with how we have acted in the past. Throughout history the church has sanctioned bigotry, misogyny, slavery, and discrimination. My goal and dream is to be a part of redeeming that message. I can't help but think that throwing away the church because it has people that are nasty, angry, or bitter is a lot like throwing away all the letters in alphabet soup. Without the people there is no church.

As a young grad student at Seattle University I had to take a multicultural education class. One of the cultures the teacher had chosen to have represented was the gay community. One of the guest speakers talked about the most difficult moment of confronting who he was and who he wanted to be. At the march on Washington he came around the corner and there was a man right in his face, screaming and angry, who yelled "God hates fags." This is the messaging that so many were raised under and millions ultimately chose their lifestyle instead of a "god" who hates them. Can you blame people for hating the church when it seemed the whole of the faith community hated them?

Similarly, the church's methods of dealing with mental illness have been particularly harsh. Even though for centuries the church was responsible for the care of those who were mentally and physically challenged, it seems the church has managed to extricate themselves from that responsibility, leaving it for others to pick up the slack. The message has been clear—this is a "them" problem—not an "us" problem.

Even more heinous is the implied guilt associated with mental illness. "Be happier. Find the joy in the Lord. The Bible says you should have peace." These verses, cherry-picked from the Bible, are spiritual bats leveraged at the spirits of the afflicted. Would I like to be happier? Yes. Would I love to find joy in everything? Yes. Do I want peace? Also yes. However, sometimes brain chemistries do not lend themselves to comprehending or processing the right emotions or feelings. Traumatic events have affected my ability to plug the proper emotions into the proper outlets. My internal emotional clock is hard-wired incorrectly. So, implying that I can just fix myself is uninformed and the very antithesis of helpful.

Additionally, this attitude places all the responsibility of healing on my ill-equipped shoulders. I believe in spiritual healing. I believe doctors, medication, and therapy can be a part of God's provision of healing. But too many times I have heard stories where churches have disregarded or degraded people afflicted with depression, anxiety, or other mental illnesses as being unfaithful and unbelieving. Even going so far as to saying that seeing therapists and taking medications are crutches, keeping people from truly believing in an all-powerful God.

My inner dialogue can be bitter and self-righteous. "You? You want me to pray. Think it through? Calm myself with talking to God? Pray YES! This is what kept me alive. This is what keeps me going. This is what gave me my survival instincts. This is what gives me strength to go out into public and interact. This is what heals my soul. I pray before I'm scared and I pray for peace in spite of fear. All the time. But don't mock my 'in the moment' need to survive. Allow me to respond instinctively, animalistically, and reactively. It is a base survival skill that God gave me. Respect that."

In 2016, I began telling my story, doling details out judiciously. But something about that felt too controlled. I was helicopter momming myself. What I really wanted was to tell my story freely with the abandon of a three-year-old flower girl flinging petals with gusto and a flourish. This slow stripping was trying my patience, so I completely disrobed. Illness, triggers, diagnosis, fears. All of it. I talked. I blogged. I put it all out there.

When Churches Are Assholes

However, I'm still afraid. I am concerned that family and friends will treat me differently than before.

But, as I have shared my story of mental illness, people have come rushing out of the fog to share their stories, like teenagers to a fresh pizza. "You're so brave," they say. "I wish we could talk about this more openly," referencing themselves or mentally ill loved ones. But even though the conversation seems to publicly resonate, I still don't feel as if it is socially acceptable to list mental ailments, especially in faith communities. It feels like a dangerous swamp filled with self-righteous alligators.

And I don't feel brave. I feel as though I'm in a sword fight with a pool noodle. I feel over-exposed and under-prepared for opinions and criticism. And vulnerable! In a world where everything from marriage, sex life, finances, and household habits are no longer sacrosanct, I am walking a tight rope between Kardashian oversharing and honesty.

I do feel everybody should get to have a "mental hospital" experience like I did, because it reminded me of how emotionally disconnected we have become. So often we act as if communities should be homogenous. Enforcing conformity makes us feel normal. However, even in the most "welcoming" communities, there are collective rules of dress, actions, vocabulary. Sameness.

My visit to the hospital, though very difficult, stands as an oasis of generosity in a desert of perceived judgment. On more than one occasion I was struck by the thought that this climate, this attitude of mutual investment and giving of gracious space, should be what church community feels like. It was in a psychiatric institution where I most clearly saw grace-in-action in the midst of the darkness.

My friends from the hospital knew their ailments, addiction, and depravity, and were talking about it, working through it. They loved in spite of labels, some of which were worn right on our name tags. From my experience, people in churches don't feel the same way. Wearing your depravity and need openly only warrants suspicion and pity, not welcome and inclusion. I fear that as a general rule my new friends would not find the church a welcome place. I get it, but I resist it. I can't help but think we can do better than this.

There is much said about how denominations, minions of the institution, control their people, and are a blight on the face of faith. However, in my situation the Evangelical Covenant Church was caring, generous, and critically helpful. They paid for a year of marriage counseling for my husband and I to try and get on the same page on a variety of issues. They paid for a therapist for me, to open the door to my trauma, past and present.

The denomination insisted I go to the workshop on trauma. They bought me a plane ticket, made lodging arrangements, and paid for the workshop.

Once the therapists felt I should be inpatient, I laughed. I did not have $65,000 to be there for the six-week protocol. The director said, "Let's just call the people who sent you here and see." The office answered on the first ring. Their response to a request to have me inpatient was met with, "Whatever she needs, we'll take care of it." I was simultaneously grateful, irritated, and terrified.

At the six-week mark the hospital wanted to extend my stay because they were still having trouble working out a treatment plan for me. My dissociative identity disorder diagnosis was a complication none of us expected so we still had more work to do. Again, when we requested extra time for me to stay, the denomination said yes.

The denomination flew two or three people out about every other month for a year or so, to check in on me, encourage me, and help me understand the realities of my situation, in relationship to my future career in the pastorate. Their graciousness, care, and generosity were an island of hope in the face of a major life shift. With their words and their actions they said, "You will have to leave this relationship before we do."

This has been a season of stillness. I have learned to find peace in the stillness because I know God is there. It is in the blackness, the quiet, and the silence that I am secure because it is where I feel the most held. There is no distraction of myself and my own feeble attempts to win the grace of One who gives it freely.

20

Girls Can Too!

IN 1998, ONE SUNDAY after I preached a sermon, I was in the sanctuary gathering my things. All of the people had left or were chatting it up in the foyer. Only one man remained. Knowing he had a volatile personality I was wary. Sure enough, he approached me. He scolded me, "How dare you preach the gospel? You're a woman!" As he got closer and closer he eventually backed me up against a wall berating me for my behavior and lack of decorum. I had no defenses. My husband and all the board members had left the room and were unaware of what was going on. Eventually the man left me by myself, shaken.

I know there are theological differences about whether or not women should be pastors. There are strong feelings on both sides of the argument. I choose not to debate the issue, having clearly made up my mind practically and theologically. However, to intimidate, shame, bully, or pressure someone to follow your particular side of any argument is just plain wrong.

The way I have always looked at this conundrum of theology is this. If I am wrong then God will judge me. However, in the process of my teaching and leading, some people have still heard the gospel, learned some about the Bible, and hopefully built a relationship with God along the way. If I am right, the same thing has happened. God's word does not ring void of its power or truth because it is proclaimed from the mouth of a woman. Also, I figure if God can use a donkey to make his point and presence known, then he can use me!

Once a male pastor said to me, "Jill. You need to be careful how you enter a room." "Why?" I asked. "Because you're beautiful, you're smart, and you're confident. It makes the wives nervous." Deeply irritated, I had the presence of mind to say, "That is not my problem. I don't dress inappropriately or act flirtatiously. If they are uncomfortable that is their problem!" I know this conversation represents a larger one. It reeks of misogyny and the old adage of " the woman as temptress." In every profession in the world women have had to fight their way through to be allowed access to the same privilege and respect that men do. This is the case even more so in the church, as opponents, many of them well meaning, wield Scripture to hold women back from primary leadership.

I was raised to believe that a woman needs to always cover themselves for the man's sake because men couldn't help themselves but look and lust. It was the woman's responsibility to care for the man's lack of self control, which is ridiculous. However, while I was working in the church I never rode in cars with male co-pastors or hardly met for coffee one on one. It was too risky for me to be seen with a male other than my husband because we might not be professionals and fall into each other's arms?

It wasn't until much later in life that I got to work in the part of the institution that understood mutual responsibility and respect. We were treated as adults with jobs to do and like the rest of the professional world were expected to act in accordance with our beliefs and high moral standards. I began to enjoy my work and thrive in it in ways that I had not before. I fell in love with being a pastor all over again. Much more can be said about the chauvinism and discrimination within the ranks of church leadership but suffice it to say that I tried to ignore the implicit and explicit bias that existed in the institution. I had a job to do, bias or not.

Starting churches is my favorite. Being a part of a team, working together to create community out of thin air is not for the faint of heart. However, it is lively, electric, and is a breath of fresh air compared to working in traditional church. By and large the rule book gets to be thrown out and the new community is a blank canvas to work with. I loved the work and challenge. It is a hard job but completely rewarding. However, it wasn't until our last church, Navigate, started in 2009 that I realized the full burden and weight of being a pastor.

Navigate was birthed out of a strong call and conviction from God to bring a church to downtown Billings. We wanted to be near Montana Avenue where both the "have" and the "have nots" converge. Our building was geographically located between the men's and women's shelters. We also were right near Montana Avenue where people with money would come to eat at nice restaurants, shop at art galleries, or go to the theater. These people would sidestep the underprivileged that sat on the stoops and streets, without acknowledging them or their plight.

To say there was trauma in our church is like saying there is jelly in a PBJ sandwich. One day one of our men, Jim, did not show up for his work. After trying to get ahold of him several times his boss, a relative of mine, called me. We went to Jim's small apartment above a garage. We banged on the door and finally broke in. The air conditioning was on full blast and the room was frigid. We found the young man lying on the couch with open pill bottles and empty bottles of alcohol strewn around the room. Even the melatonin and vitamin C bottles were empty. When the EMTs got there the situation looked dire. It looked as if he was gone. Jim had no family in the area so I followed them to the hospital and sat while they pumped his stomach.

The doctors instructed me to call his family, because they doubted he was going to live much longer. I found his mother's number and made the call no mother wants to hear. "Your son is going to die." Her stunned silence spoke loudly. However, Jim did make it. It was a miracle. His air conditioning had kept his body temperature low enough that it slowed all the functions in his body. It couldn't process all the drugs and alcohol he took. He was beyond fortunate. Because his family couldn't afford to fly to see him, I sat for days with him in the ICU, waiting for him to wake up.

To love someone as their pastor is to care about their emotional, physical, relational, and spiritual health. It is to desire to see their whole self thrive to the point of being able to help others find the same kind of hope. So, to watch a parishioner stare death in the face, is to watch your love slipping away. Eventually Jim was glad to be alive and it proved to be a turning point in getting his life straightened out.

On a lighter note, one day Chance came to church. He was a well-known drag queen in the area and friends with some of our people. For a long time he insisted he couldn't come into church because if he did it would burst into flames! I asked him, "Chance, are you ever going to come to church in drag?" He said emphatically, "Jill. You don't know what it takes to get up, shave, put on makeup, fix your hair and get all dressed up!" I looked up at him and said, "Do you think I just wake up looking this pretty?!"

Post-Traumatic Faith

A member of our congregation got visibly shook up and kind of nasty when a visitor walked in. Later I inquired about her reaction. The response shocked me. "We were in the same swingers club. I have naked pictures of her!!!" My first response was, "Get rid of the damn pictures." And then told her that if somebody wanted to come to the church we would welcome them with open arms, unless they are a threat to someone's safety. She needed to put that lifestyle in her past and move forward.

One morning just before church I heard that Judy, who lived at the women and children's shelter, was being taken by ambulance to the hospital. I finished service and went to the hospital. She was battered and claimed she had fallen. She clearly had not. She had been beaten. Her husband would not let me in the room and didn't want anybody to talk to him or treat her. He checked her out of the hospital and I never saw them again.

It wasn't an unusual thing for me to get a collect call from the local jail, often times on Sunday morning. On Sundays I wouldn't take the calls but I could search the local registry to see which of my parishioners had managed to get themselves locked up. Good times.

The drama and trauma continued throughout the course of the life of the church. And I appreciated it because it meant people were showing who they really were, not masking and covering up their real lives.

We were a hodgepodge of people. Catholics, Protestants, atheists. It was a multicultural congregation: Native American, Puerto Rican, Korean, Black, and Caucasian. Artists, health care workers, pilots, musicians, homeless living in cars, and a contingency from the shelters.

I loved teaching and caring for our little congregation. I cooked, cried, counseled, and celebrated with them. We lived life together and I didn't do everything right, but I did love them.

In 2015, after I left the hospital, to my deep, deep grief and palpable sorrow, my church closed because I couldn't pastor it anymore. The stress of the job was too much and I was mentally fragile.

My psychiatrist said very clearly to me, "Jill! You can never run into that burning building again. Your time responding to crisis is done." I cried wretched tears over the people I loved and missed so deeply, longing to explain to them what happened to me, even though I barely understood it myself.

I miss Navigate with my whole heart. Not having that church is a lot like a phantom limb. I can still feel it even though it is gone. Sometimes it hurts, even though it isn't there.

21

Mosquitos and Lord Ladimore

THE HOSPITAL/CLINIC WAS ESTABLISHED on some lovely grounds. Well manicured, thick grass, outdoor pool, and a wide variety of trees and plants lulled first-time visitors into its picturesque setting. I suppose the grounds could certainly be seen symbolically as a sort of oasis in the middle of the desert. However, I hate the desert. Give me deciduous trees and four seasons any day. In 100+ degrees of heat I am basically a cactus: prickly and everything about me says *go away*!

However, an unpublicized fact about these lush surroundings is they are a breeding ground for mosquitos. It seemed every mosquito in the tri-state area had discovered this posh little getaway. I could not step outside of the buildings for 30 seconds without getting bit. One evening I was so desperate for fresh air that I spray painted myself in bug repellent. I am pretty sure there was a Jill-sized dry spot, like a crime scene outline, left in the middle of a bug spray lake right there in the nursing station entryway! Fully saturated, I confidently sloshed my way to the great outdoors. I was out no less than two minutes before I got bitten. Those aggressive little vermin climbed up my pants and bit me five times on my ass. This may have been an oasis but it was also a mosquito hostel. Holy hell.

While at the hospital a resident, Serena, came with her support animal, a beautiful German shepherd, Serbie. The dog was well loved but not well trained. More than once she lunged at another resident who got too close to her owner. Serena was a psychiatrist who had been released from her residency. Hundreds of thousands of dollars in debt and without a residency, her prospects looked bleak.

Serena liked to wear onesie costumes with ears on the hoods. Serbie had matching onesies. One day in the art room Serena was frustrated with her treatment at the hospital. "They treat us like we're crazy!" she said in frustration. Another resident said matter-of-factly, "Well. You are in a psych hospital. In a onesie. With a dog. In a matching onesie!" Highly indignant, Serena marched out and left us to our art.

Animals were always a source of joy for me. Throughout the years I had a fair number of them. The one rule about naming animals was, since our last name began with L, Llafet, all the animals had to be named with an L. While in Nevada we had Laurie, the German shepherd that I only know through pictures (she died before I came around).

One Easter, my mother, an animal lover herself, spontaneously decided to buy me some ducks and chickens. We went to the pet store and I got two yellow fluffy chickens and two downy baby ducks. We put them in a pen left by the previous owner in our back yard. I named the chickens Lolli and Lollipop. The ducks, who somehow seemed regal, were named Lord Ladimore and Lady Lulu.

We already had cats crowned King Louis and Queen Louisa so the ducks were lower down the pecking order. I loved the birds. I would play with them on the grass. On warm summer days all four of them would crawl up my bell bottom corduroy pants and we would all fall asleep in the sun in the front yard. We celebrated when the chickens laid their first teeny tiny eggs.

Lemon the parakeet was kind of a pain in the ass. When she would flutter her wings seed hulls would fly everywhere. She was a mess all the time. I can't say I was too disappointed when I found her dead in her cage one morning.

Marilyn bought a rescue dog for me. He was a black and white midsize mutt. I adored him. Lacking creativity, I named him Lollipop, because I couldn't think of another "L" name. Lollipop was strong and when he would take off, while on leash, he would drag me across the yard. I got hurt several times before Marilyn got rid of him. In his place I received a small child's tea set with pictures of a black dog painted on the pieces. I still have the tea set but always felt sad about not getting to keep the dog.

My favorite were the cats. King Louis, a black and white cat, was docile and compliant to all things kids. We used to dress him up and put him in doll beds where he would just curl up and take a nap. Louis rode in our bicycle baskets, around our necks, or even over jumps, never flinching.

The princess, Queen Louisa, was prissy as my sister, Dana'. Girly, particular, and in charge. A beautiful all white cat, she usually wanted nothing to do with the kids. But occasionally, she did let us dress her up in dolly clothes. We rocked her to sleep in doll cradles with King Louis.

22

I'm Batman

WHILE IN THE PSYCH and trauma hospital we were cut off from the outside world except for an occasional call made through circa 1970s phones and letters. It is an odd thing not to have a cell phone with you. I could deal with the absence of phone calls, text messages, and emails. What was really odd is to have conversations, try and describe yourself, without proof of life—photos of family, business cards, and pictures of yourself working and recreating. We are so accustomed to showing our life rather than telling about it. Words to describe our lives are in short supply and images are in high demand. I couldn't wait until my first box from home arrived because I had requested pictures of my family. I needed that connection to the outside world. Without it I was completely alone and anonymous in the crowd of patients.

Once evening addiction meetings were finished, they allowed us to use the corded touch button phones. (I did have to show a twenty-year-old how to use the phone and phone card. Kids these days.) A list would start and when it was their turn, each person would use their phone card to punch in thirty-six numbers to reach the outside world. We had five minutes to reassure our loved ones and ourselves that all would be okay. While we waited for the phone we would sit and eat popcorn, fruit, trail mix, ice cream, or whatever snacks the kitchen provided for the evening.

Due to not having access to phones or computers we were mostly blind to the outside world. There were newspapers on the breakfast table for those who wanted to read but our own lives were sensational enough that there was no other news most of us could handle. People who did read mostly read the gossip rags, comics, and the stock market. No news was important enough to interrupt even our reverie of bad, caffeine-free coffee and pancakes with sugar-free syrup.

However, the nurses would let us watch TV most Saturdays and Sundays. For the football lovers this was glorious since it was fall. For non-athletic supporters it was not. There was at least one occasion when the arm chair quarterbacks left the room, we pounced on the remote, and changed the television to some "chick" movie. When they returned, a war broke out, which I think amounted to hostile words, idle threats, and football. My children wondered what happened to me. I arrived at the hospital an occasional football fan, mostly coerced by my husband, but returned home a ripened fan, yelling at the TV, refs, and whomever else would listen.

My whole family was caught off guard by my hospitalization. People often ask me what my husband and children did while I was inpatient and could only talk occasionally. The fact is I only know what they did based on shadowy reflections they or other people tell me. Overnight all of their routines and schedules had to be changed. They all had to adjust to a one-parent household. From what they tell me, the children all reacted differently. The younger two sought out their "other moms." We have always been blessed with a community of families with whom our children felt at home. Some of those other moms stepped in during this time to cook dinner, bake, or hang out with the girls. Our son spent a lot of time in the basement, when he wasn't in school or playing percussion in band. He drew into himself and pushed down the confused feelings. Our oldest was in the Air Force, which was difficult for all of us, since we couldn't call her easily and she couldn't call us on any predictable schedule.

My husband kept himself busy and distracted by catching up on house projects and just trying to keep the kids together. It was a horrific time for all of us.

Doctors and staff worked for months to unlock the complexities of my mind and emotions. Multiple "methodologies" were used to help me get in touch with my inner child; equine therapy with ancient horses, ropes course, art therapy, yoga, tai chi, meditation, brain wave analysis, light therapy, spiritual reflection, and countless hours of talk therapy. While the institution is paid good money to help its clients find a healthier and more fulfilling life, the approach is to first shed light on the ugly parts of ourselves. It was tortuous. What more could I expect from a $10,000 a week "hotel" that banned caffeine past 8 a.m. and sugar at all times. "Stay away from sugar and caffeine, kids. They are mood altering chemicals. Feel free to contemplate that over your morning cigarette."

One of the only bright spots of hanging out in a psych center was the weekly outing to the ropes course. The change of scenery from the quarter square mile campus was delicious. Getting to go was a privilege, reserved for those deemed medically and mentally sound, which meant most patients didn't get permission for at least four weeks. They wanted to make sure we wouldn't try to hang ourselves on the ropes or jump out of the van and run into McDonalds or Subway, like caffeine- and sugar-deprived crazies.

At the hospital, we piled into vans with all the excitement of kids going to summer camp. My first week on the course I tried rock-wall climbing. Some of the younger and more athletic among us crawled up the wall like frickin' Spiderman. I was more amoeba, blob-like, as I sauntered up the wall at a snail's pace. I was thrilled to have two full grown men belay, counterbalance, for me. As evidenced by their sweat rings I'm sure they worked harder to get my ass up to the first level of the wall than I did. The two worn-out men on the other end of my rope didn't have enough energy or breath support to encourage me to go further. A beleaguered thumbs up, and they let me float myself down the hard-fought ten feet I had climbed.

My third trip to the ropes course was on Halloween. I sported Batman glasses and a cape that a friend had sent me and was determined to conquer the obstacle before me. I climbed up a thirty-foot pole, jumped off the platform the size and stability of a saltine cracker, and caught a rope loop with one foot that was ten feet away. Then I swung fifty feet, at five-foot intervals, catching my feet in the rope loops as I went. I sweated, swung, and swore all the way to the last loop.

At the end I gave one last mighty swing and caught the last platform with my foot. However, instead of sticking the landing I ended up strung out, like roast chicken on a spit, horizontally suspended thirty feet in the air, belly and cape flapping in the wind for the world to see—one foot clinging to the platform, my hands clinging to the guide rope.

To make matters worse, I had shoes with no shoe laces and gravity was threatening to separate me from my shoe. As I mentally negotiated my next move, I lost my shoe and was beginning to lose my pants. My only hope for modesty was the harness, which, though chafing, was keeping the proper parts covered. But I pulled through and made it. My triumph? After resituating my pants, I jumped off that platform, cape flying, and landed brilliantly on the ground, on one foot, just like Batman.

23

Pac-Man Sucks

THREE TIMES A WEEK, for approximately twenty minutes a day, I had treatment in the brain center, a small, white, stucco building in the center of the complex. The technician would attach one electrode to my earlobe and one to the top of my head, using some kind of gritty lotion. After they hooked me up to the computer, each of my delta, theta, and alpha waves appeared on the monitor, represented in different colors of squiggling, moving lines. It was amazing to watch and discover I actually had active brain waves, which I very much doubted by this point. The goal of the brain center was to be able to see the brain waves freak out when anxiety crept in, and then regulate myself.

They introduced a variety of games to help me monitor my internal stress and anxiety. First I tried a simplified version of *Pac-Man*, where calmness made the yellow blob go and overanxious brain waves made him stop. Then I tried the skateboarder, where she fell off her board and crashed if my brain was going too fast or too slow. They tried a cruise liner where you helped the boat get to an island by encouraging it with calm thoughts. A hot air balloon would stay afloat, encouraged by calm brain waves. I had dismal results. Pac-Man refused to move, the skateboarder ran into everything, and my damn ship never did reach its destination.

My internal dialogue was something like: "Okay. Calm. Breathe. Relax. Wait?! Why won't you move you freakin' little. . . . Calm. Breathe. Breathe slower. I hate this game. I hate it. I hate it. I . . . okay. You got this. . . . *Oh my word*. I've always disliked skateboards. . . . Is my time up yet? Damn. Only ten seconds used up. . . . I have an itch. I wonder if there is peanut butter in the cafeteria. I think it's my butt that itches. Oops. I have gas. The sugar substitute stuff gives me gas. Oh, skateboarder . . . right. You're still sitting on the ground. Hope that hurt your ass when you fell. . . . Calm. Your time is almost up. *What*? I have another two thirty-second intervals to go?"

I felt as if my charted brain waves would be more useful to predict a seismic anomaly than for calming my anxiety. But eventually, I became a little more focused and a lot less spastic about this state-of-the-art therapy. Now there are days I would love to have a screen in front of me to tell me if my brain is racing, anxious, or spastic.

The art room was an interesting diversion from the regular group talk therapy. A small and ever-revolving group of us spent a great deal of time there. The room, while inviting, was sparsely stocked with supplies. They provided old magazines for collages, paints, paper, crayons, clay, and markers. A thin magnet strip held art from residents, displaying skill levels from those who really stunk at art to those who could make a living at it. A square table sucked up all the space in the center of the room, leaving only walking room around it. We sat and painted or sculpted clay. One night a group decided to do makeup demonstrations on each other. A tattoo artist sat and drew detailed gothic lettered signs and crosses. A friend put a large piece of paper in the center of the table and lay down on it. I climbed up on the table and traced her body shape for a project she was working on with her therapist. A few steps away from the main room, there was a small room for storage and a basin for washing paint brushes. That tiny closet room was one of the only spots on campus free of oversight, monitoring, or video cameras. It was reportedly one of the places people would sneak in a quickie on campus.

The art therapist in the hospital was surprisingly serious and disappointingly nonplayful. I wanted her to be jovial and burst alive in her creativity. However, through her work I was reminded that art can be a great outlet and expression for things that cannot be said. This may be why I have spent the whole of my life creating things. Knitting, quilting, scrapbooking, jewelry making, beading, stamping, coloring, embroidery, photography, and music. I invest my free time in "making stuff." Some hobbies stick and some are just fun, fleeting adventures. However, with every effort I find myself learning something new and hopefully creating a little extra beauty in the world.

Pac-Man Sucks

One day the art therapist instructed the class to create their internal monster out of modeling clay. We were to put shape and form to the internal battle within us. Lois, a very crabby seventy-year-old, was in class. Lois would follow me around campus saying, "What are you even doing here? You seem fine. Go home! You don't even look sick." Lois rolled her clay into a long snake and coiled it up neatly. When it came time for everybody to describe their art, the very sweet, well-meaning, art therapist asked Lois. "Does that represent your father coiled and ready to strike out in anger at you?" "NO!" she snapped. "It represents the easiest thing to make with clay!"

Patient 1
Therapist 0

24

Suicide Surges

IN HIGH SCHOOL, IN the late 1980s, I was desperate and suicidal. I saw no possibility that anything in my life would change. Marilyn had started talking about moving to wherever I went to college. There was no escaping her. She was a boa strangling the will, freedom, and fight out of me.

I considered taking a bunch of pills, but we only had Tylenol and Ibuprofen. I couldn't imagine those could kill anybody. There were no firearms in the house for me to use so that wasn't an option. The only option I could come up with was a knife. I wasn't sure I could handle that kind of pain. That left only one option, murder. I did not want her to exist or be part of my life. I imagined repeatedly stabbing her in her sleep, which would be the only way she wouldn't overpower me. Somehow I convinced myself that somebody would understand that I was abused and exonerate me for my crime should I decide to kill her. I remember watching the story of the Menendez brothers killing of their parents in 1989 and wondered, if they got away for killing their parents with cause, perhaps that possibility existed for me. I never attempted either plan but the emotions still existed. And the Menendez brothers are still in prison.

The hospital was serious about suicidal thoughts and ideations. First thing they did was take away anything that we could strangle, stab, or cut with. Then, ironically, they gave us a name tag/lanyard to hang around our neck, to be worn at all times. They must not have thought I was a threat to myself. They allowed me to have my hair dryer and curling irons, also contraband for those in the way of self harm, because of their cords. Nurses watched closely as we swallowed meds, to make sure we didn't stash them anywhere to "share" with others. There was no bathtub drain to ensure that I wouldn't drown myself. However, it occurred to me that one tuck and roll down the hill and I could drown myself in the outdoor pool.

"Have you ever been suicidal? Are you a danger to yourself?" In mental health care these questions become disturbingly familiar. One of the doctor's statements rattled around my head like marbles in a tin can. "With your diagnosis you will feel suicidal at least a couple more times in your life."

We aren't really supposed to talk about suicide. It is the deepest of the dark secrets. To admit that you are so lost and feel as if you are ruining so many peoples' lives is demoralizing. To stand in that place weighing the decision of whether to live or die is soul shattering. If you survive, the internal wrestling match itself leaves emotionally scorched earth. For someone with experience and knowledge to tell me that I will be there again was jolting.

During the last two weeks of my extended stay at the hospital, the clinicians arranged for a phone call with my boss. Ignorant as to the nature of the call, I assumed it was just a check-in to see how I was doing. Because I thought very highly of my boss, I gladly took the call at the arranged time. To my surprise, my boss's supervisor was also on the call. "We have looked into the finances of your church," they said. "There seem to be some irregularities. We are calling to ask about some of your books." They asked about receipts and expenditures, line item by line item, roughly twenty different entries. I explained each one and what it was for, growing more and more distressed. "Well," they continued. "We think it is actionable and have elevated it for review by the board." I collapsed emotionally, my body felt numb and cold. Any emotional skeleton I had left to hold me up fell, twisted into a heap.

They thought I was a thief. They were questioning my character. I had been away from my children for ten weeks. I was seeking separation from my husband. I wouldn't be able to work once released so I would lose the church I loved with all my heart. I had spent two months processing trauma after trauma from my childhood. And now? Now I didn't even have my character anymore. With the stain of their accusations, I could feel the hopelessness and blackness closing in.

I wanted to die. I thought, "My children will be better off without this lump of a human as a mother and no one will miss me." The chaperone for my phone call alerted hospital staff about the severity of my sudden downturn. I was placed on suicide watch and pumped with more medication for my anxiety. I tearfully and obligingly did what they wanted, but I didn't care what attempt they made to treat me or bolster my will to live. I was done.

The psychiatric physicians assistant met me on the sidewalk and saw I was so sad and was crying. She had anxiety meds added to my regiment. She talked with me and told me the suicide rates among children whose parents commit suicide are extraordinarily high. "You don't have the right to this decision. You are a parent." To be reminded of that was anchoring.

"Arm-to-arm care" is what they call suicide watch. My nurse's aide could not be physically more than an arm's length away from me. They kept the bathroom doors open, we sat side by side at meals, they escorted me to every class. She sat outside therapy rooms waiting for me to be done with my appointments and I slept with someone sitting by my bed, watching me every minute of the night. I wasn't allowed to leave campus with the group for ropes course or equine therapy. I wasn't allowed to shave and the contents of my room were once more scrutinized.

To be on that level of care and watched so closely is disconcerting and, I suppose, to a balanced mind, demoralizing. But at that moment, nothing mattered except darkness and my desire to sink into it.

Severe depression and suicidality are blinders against all hope. They block out light and confuse the senses. Surreal. Terrifying. Disconcerting. You feel the confusion of invisibility, nothingness, and at the same time feel as if your heart weighs a thousand pounds. It is to feel the full responsibility of the world tied to you like a ticking bomb and know you are powerless to escape it. All the failures and faults of your life are laid out before you and the verdict is in. You mean nothing. You are nothing and will not be missed. You have failed at what every other person you know has accomplished; just being a basic good human. The sick brain makes suicide an act of sacrifice, surrender, and mercy for those who had to deal with you. In the darkness there are no acceptable answers. No choice is good.

In a week, I rallied in time to convince them to release me. Looking back, they should not have because I was still a threat to myself. But I won them over and they let me go home. I told them I had to remember what I was fighting for. I needed to see my kids.

After I was released, my bosses apologized profusely and begged for my forgiveness. But the blow dealt to my confidence and character has been devastating. I still feel the burn of their accusation in my soul and cannot brush it away.

Someday it may become dark again but I'm hoping when it does, this work I am doing will have opened doors to relationships with others with whom I can be completely honest. I'm hoping. I want that for myself and for so many others.

25

Multiplied Me

I HAVE TRIED TO keep one part of my mental health diagnosis to myself, but like a fart on an airplane, it was going to reveal itself eventually.

I have dissociative identity disorder (DID), formerly known as multiple personality disorder. I fear sharing this diagnosis because it is shrouded in stigma and misperception. So much (mis)understanding of DID comes from mainstream media. Hollywood stories like *Split*, *Three Faces of Eve*, *United States of Tara*, and *Primal Fear*[1] give a one-dimensional view into the lives of those of us who have this adaptation in their brains. In these stories each of the main character's personalities has a distinctive language pattern, way of dressing, mannerisms, and habits. The switch from personality to personality is dramatic and quite outwardly visible. Often the main character of the shows are sociopathic and dangerous. While this can certainly be true for some people managing life with DID, it is not true for all. My own experience does not mirror those stories. It's important to remember that it's Hollywood that has stigmatized these disorders, not the sufferers within the mental health community.

How does this happen? It has taken me years of reading and research to begin to understand the complexities of a mind, my mind, where this adaptation happens. From the best of my understanding a mind splits when a person is in a dire, inescapable, and life-threatening circumstance. In a

---

1. Universal, 2016; 20th Century Fox, 1957; Showtime, 2009–11; Paramount, 1996.

situation where there is no ability to fight back or flee to safety, the brain can keep the emotions of the victim safe by building up a wall to keep the circumstances quarantined from the rest of the brain. This is the creation of separate states, parts, or people in a brain. DID is most commonly linked with childhood abuse and neglect, when a brain is the most pliable. There are several types of dissociation, all of which are safety valves for sufferers of abuse and/or neglect. By dissociating a person is failing to integrate their whole self—emotions, personality, physical sensation—creating a rigid box that stores the bad experience, allowing them to live in a reality where that particular pain does not exist.

Splitting off into other protective "personalities" acts as insurance that the overall brain stays intact and can survive. It is a miraculous gift to be able to insulate my mind this way. My psychiatrist said I stored trauma like books on a shelf. Every trauma that happened I packed it up and put it on the shelf. "Now the shelf has broken and you have a mess everywhere and we have to figure out how to clean it up," he said.

It has been a journey for me to accept that diagnosis. I'll admit, when I first heard it, I felt intrinsically damaged. I felt marked and labeled, poked and prodded like some circus exhibit. The bearded lady, the contortionist, the elephant man, and Jill. I was fearful I would never be allowed in polite society again.

The ability to dissociate becomes a clinical problem when my dissociation is frequent and keeps me from interacting in the present. It can keep me from processing or acknowledging difficult memories. It is an involuntary response like coughing or a reflex knee jerk.

It is a running joke in my family that my memory often misfires or doesn't fire at all. The truth of it is, sometimes I can't remember what was said or done during a dissociative episode because my brain was not functioning in the present. Eight months ago, I enjoyed dinner out with my family and friends to celebrate my birthday. Recently, I mentioned to my youngest that we really need to take her to that particular restaurant someday. She reminded me we had gone for my birthday. I have no recollection, zero memory, of having done this.

Dissociation also affects how I view past events. When I watch home movies and look at pictures of times with my children growing up, I visually and cognitively register that it is me in the pictures. However, I have no memory, feeling, or recollection of having been there. There are no warm fuzzies at pictures of me with their little faces, joy at the sound of their baby voices, or deep sighs for time gone by. The memories are mirages with no substance or foundation. It's as if I am watching an actor on screen who happens to look exactly like me. It is a detachment between what I see and what I feel.

For me, dissociation is an involuntary escaping to something or escaping to nothing at all. Dissociation is a way of mentally exiting an uncomfortable reality, circumstance, thought, or memory. It feels like a camera lens, zooming reality in and out, with darkness creeping in from all sides. It can feel like zoning out while hyper-fixating on some object, face, or spot on the floor. Blissful, quiet, unfocused fuzziness, leaning over the edge of the present, gazing at the past.

One night, during the first few weeks of my stay at the psych/trauma hospital I went on a surprise midnight adventure. I got out of bed, put on my bathrobe, and left my room. The next day the charge nurse said my door alarm, indicating I had left my room, went off but nobody bothered to check it. There should have been a nurse at the nurse's station but I walked past their empty post and out of the building. The outer door alarm also failed to arouse any investigation. The nurse expressed how deeply sorry they were about failing to protect me. They probably sensed a pending lawsuit and wanted to make sure I felt safe now. Since I remembered very little about it, I forgave their negligence, but at my request, I slept with my door open for a couple of nights. I wanted to make sure I was where I was supposed to be. I was terrified of wandering out again unintentionally.

My flickering memories of those two hours are of sitting on cement stairs in between some buildings, the sound of vehicles whizzing by and water splashing in a fountain. The nurse's notes reflect that I returned to the nurse's station two hours later, which startled and alarmed them since I was supposed to be sound asleep in my room. What happened and why could I not remember clearly? I had a dissociative event.

It wasn't the last dissociative event I had while I was there. At one point I was terrified to come out of my room because I thought I heard gunfire. Another time I found myself on the sidewalk in socks, with nurses around me talking to me about how I shouldn't wander around in stocking feet in the desert. Nurses notes reveal that I wandered out a handful of times and was coaxed back into my room. I'm not sure how they bribed me to go back to my room, but it certainly wasn't with coffee and chocolate cake. Damn sugar-free campus.

Multiplied Me

Dissociation can also be retreating into other parts of myself. My brain can feel as if I am seeing life through a child's eyes, or a teenager—different iterations of myself that live within my fractured mind. Each part has distinctive needs, wants, and expressions of who they are. I have made the intentional decision to not try and integrate all my "parts." For me, each part holds a different set of memories and was created for a purpose, to protect. To decide to pursue an integrated life, one where all the parts of me live as a single brain with a singular set of memories, seems not only intangible but also unwise. Why would I want to tear down the walls that my mind created to protect me? I would rather befriend them than dissolve them all into each other like Jell-O in hot water.

Part of what made this diagnosis so scary is that I did not know one other person who suffered from C-PTSD, DID, and their frustrating bedfellows of depression and anxiety. People with these diagnoses don't generally come out of the dark because history tells us people with mental illness are not welcome—especially with something as unusual as DID. We tend to label people who suffer from mental illness, insisting they hide their diagnosis in closets and back rooms, beneath clothes that don't fit, dusty luggage, and out of season sporting equipment. But I need to talk about this. I need others who will too. I need to share my story so that someday someone will feel a little less weird and a lot less hopeless about their life.

It's a challenging way to live. DID makes reading books difficult because I can't remember characters from one chapter to the next. My husband says every movie is new to me because I don't remember how they end, which is true sometimes. I considered pursuing the next level of education but I decided I could not do it as I can't remember days, details, and content that I would need to achieve a doctoral degree.

One day I heard that my little grandmother had died months previous. I was furious. Why did nobody tell me? Then a day later, still stewing, I felt a flicker of a memory in the back of my mind. I looked back in my journals to find I had written a piece about her death. I had blocked it out of my memory. Recently I thought "I haven't heard from Marie (a wonderful family friend) in quite some time." I checked her Facebook, which she kept active on, and discovered she had died some two years prior. I had forgotten completely.

Living with DID is a challenge because my brain is constantly battling a nonexistent enemy and escaping to higher ground, leaving me in the darkness. You would never know my brain is checking in and out. I cannot predict when it will happen and often don't even know when it has, until I cannot remember something I did this day, week, or last month. All I know is that it happens frequently, daily.

This is living with a DID brain; a lot of blank space with fragments of memory floating around like puzzle pieces anxiously looking for a match to make a more complete picture.

Many years ago we took the children to Disneyland. One of my favorite rides was Soarin' Over California. You are placed in chairs in front of a big screen and then through Disney magic it feels as if you are hang-gliding over oceans, mountains, and forests all over California. While I enjoyed it immensely, it felt out of control, dizzying, and disconcerting. I had to look over to the side of the room occasionally to get my grounding and remind myself that I wasn't actually going to fall into the ocean or off the mountain. Often I have to do this to combat dissociative episodes. I have to remind myself that what I feel is not reality. I ground myself to the current place and time.

I didn't choose this. I didn't choose my abusive, cruel parents. I can look at this with eyes filled with tears that say "it's not fair" and "I am ruined." I don't like waking with horrible nightmares or flashbacks of crimes against my child self. However, over the years I have "settled" and come to terms with my diagnosis. My conclusion is that I am so grateful that God has protected me for decades in more ways than I could even imagine. Dissociation saved me so I have embraced it. Most days.

It's funny. Comments were made to me by other patients at the hospital about how long I was there and how I didn't even seem to need to be in the hospital. However, I had to be in longer than any other person I know. I nearly tied the record for length of stay at that particular institution. I had to stay because the clinicians had trouble diagnosing and getting me to acclimate and begin to understand my diagnosis of dissociative identity disorder.

There is a phrase I learned. "Keep your side of the street clean." Which is to say, take care of your business and let others take care of theirs. I know there are those who know me who will find this particular piece of my diagnosis to be controversial, falsified, or fictitious. All I can say is that I will keep my side of the street clean by continuing treatment and avenues that help me not only understand myself but also live in community well. I only pray that my description, experience, and understanding of this adaptation in the brain finds ground that is open to grace, learning, and understanding.

26

Christmas Cactus

BEFORE GOING TO THE hospital in 2015 I had never seen a psychiatrist. They are a funny bunch. The first one I met in the hospital was straight-talking, direct, and warm. In fact, I didn't even know she was assessing me as we talked. For all I knew, we were one sugar cube away from a tea party. Her humor, candor, and attentiveness put me at ease in a place where I was terribly uncomfortable. The world of psychiatry being a foreign landscape to me left me feeling confused and on high alert—not sure if something bad were about to happen. She was able to dial those feelings down a notch or two during our short time together.

Then I saw the stern, seasoned Baptist. I wasn't sure what to expect from him but he was affable and kind. His office was lined with books. One day, longing for something to read besides the educational and self-help assigned reading, I asked to borrow a book of poems. He did not let me. Later, in his notes I read, "She was trying to manipulate the situation by asking to borrow books." Asshole.

This doctor introduced me to the world of introspection. What was I feeling? Why did I feel that way? What can I do to change it? What is my responsibility to take care of and what is others' responsibility to manage? From he and the other therapists I learned what boundaries were and what having good self esteem was all about. I discovered that I had no self esteem that wasn't attached to my job or my children. I had no space for self esteem that was "just because I'm me." I saw no value in just being me.

Post-Traumatic Faith

Upon returning home to Billings, Montana, I saw a psychiatrist who talked at the ceiling through his eyelids and looked like Dr. Spock. He was extremely intelligent. We managed to talk about books, social issues, philosophers, and all sorts of things while diving deep into my trauma and need for psychiatric help for the rest of my life.

After Spock retired there was the quirky, effervescent, flappy-hands doctor who also liked to talk to his eyelids. He was a genius in medications and finally got me on a regiment that allowed me to sleep, avoid nightmares, manage depression and anxiety, and tolerate normal situations in life. He was deeply conversant and helped me feel safe to express details of my life that nobody on the planet had heard.

Finally, there is the psychiatrist who looks like Q in the James Bond films. He is soft-spoken and truly curious as to my mental state but not therapeutic in our conversations. However, he is encouraging about my therapy, curious about dissociation, and conservative about changing any medication regimen.

I have eyed each of them with the curiosity of a vegetarian eyeballing a hamburger—trepidatiously and with some concern as to whether I would outlive the experience. Happily, I have survived them all. Coincidentally, all the psychiatrists have had a Christmas cactus in their office. I now have one too, on the outside chance that it possesses some magic key to unlocking and healing the inner mind.

Every psychiatrist I have seen has told me, "You will not come back well from another breakdown." I'm not exactly sure what that means, but if it means I would feel more fragile than I do now, I respectfully decline the offer. So I do all the things in my control to prevent that from happening, including but not limited to regulating the amount of sleep I get, diminishing my stress by working less and declining projects that will keep me high on adrenaline and tight deadlines, going to trauma therapy twice a week, and taking a significant number of medications.

Psychiatric medication is helpful and lifesaving but sometimes it feels like juggling knives blindfolded. Something can always go wrong and there are so many moving parts that it's hard to know which is the problem. But every day I take anti-depressants, pills to help the anti-depressants, anti-psychotics, three kinds of anti-anxiety meds, blood pressure meds to keep the nightmares at bay, and sleep meds to help me go to sleep and stay asleep. *And* a rescue med to calm me down when nothing else is working. It's a lot.

Christmas Cactus

For years now, medications have flitted in and out of my life at an alarming rate. Under doctor's supervision, I keep trying them on for size to see what is the best fit. It's like the worst kind of kissing booth at the fair. Some of the meds are friendly and others are saboteurs. Some prospects are wonderful while others are completely unfortunate looking, sloppy, and lack manners.

I have a bucket of medication, under my bed, that I have acquired over the last seven years of complex-PTSD treatment. I'm fairly certain I could earn a fortune selling little goodie bags of my drugs on the street. On one hand, I am opposed to taking a bunch of pills in the same way that I am opposed to bras, traffic signals, and politicians. Necessary evils to put an unbalanced world right. On the other hand, I am grateful for proper medications because they give me the quality of life that at one time I didn't think was possible. This is the dance of medication.

Even with all the support I have, there are days when I feel as if I can't manage to get out of the house and interact with the world. There are also days when I feel as if I can "Tony the tiger" and catch the world by its tail. No one day is like another, except every day feels the same.

Frequently I feel like dumping the thousands of dollars worth of medications into the garbage and going commando, living life free of them. Other days there aren't enough meds in the world to curb the anxiety and frustrations of life. Sometimes by the end of the day I begin to mentally play Russian roulette, trying to decide if I take a little extra of this or that, can I get to sleep and end my day faster? I don't, but it does cross my mind.

I'm a gyroscope on a roller-coaster. My sense of balance and orientation is dependent on the correct combination of sleep, food, activity, inactivity, interaction, solitude, spiritual balance and, of course, meds. If even one of those things is out of balance I feel as though I will hurtle off the track and go crashing to the ground.

In 2014 I had my first therapist appointment in Billings. Gayle was close to retirement age, and experience had aged her to perfection like fine art. Gayle was kind, engaging, and a careful listener. As we dipped a toe into some of my childhood trauma I could feel her alarm growing. When we finally circled around to the issue of sexual abuse she was flabbergasted that I had never really talked about it. Those timid disclosures were the cracked door to me sharing my full history. The more we talked, the more I became aware of the unraveling that was happening in my tangled, busy, messy life.

Post-Traumatic Faith

She encouraged me to find deeper trauma help than she could provide. I ended up going to the hospital soon after that.

When I went to the hospital I received a trauma therapist. His office had a Native American motif, with small rock collections, feathers, and dream catchers scattered throughout. He was an enigma to me. I didn't know how or what to communicate to a trauma therapist! His favorite phrase was "notice that." Every time something in our conversation triggered me and I would move my hand or head, as a reaction to our conversation, he would bring it to my attention with "notice that." He helped me understand the mind-body connection and how we could change the body's reaction to trauma through intentionally healing the traumatized mind first.

This wonderful, Buddhist, evolutionist, Native American trauma therapist said to me one day, "Jill, whatever primordial pool your ancestors crawled out of—*you* were made to survive." I agree. I absolutely was made to survive. With the help of my faith and God, my spirit has been able to withstand many difficult circumstances. And sometimes, in an almost inaudible scary Batman voice I say, "*You will not kill me*" to myself, just in case any of my internal or external enemies feel the need to try and take me out.

We wore name tags around the hospital campus. The labels had our first name and initial of our last name. Colored dots were put on the name tags to signify which therapeutic group we were assigned. I was in the silver group. Special dietary or behavioral restrictions were also placed on tags. For instance, if a patient were not to interact with people of the opposite gender, this was denoted on their name tag. Armed with this information, we were able to identify with some specificity one another's trouble area. The red group dealt with anger, the green one addiction, and the silver one trauma. However, I felt I didn't really need a badge to identify who I was. My own nonreturnable diagnosis felt much like a forehead tattoo, always on display. I had all the insecurity of a teenage girl with a fresh batch of zits.

There were too many residents named Jason in the hospital. It was confusing so the residents renamed them all. One extraordinarily handsome man from Memphis was just called "Memphis." A particularly jolly bloke, for some nondescript reason, chose the name "Bubbles." Another Jason showed up wearing a police GPS and alcohol ankle monitor on. We just called him "Tracker." And one lucky man got to remain "Jason."

On Monday of my first week in the hospital, at 10 in the morning, I made my way to the building beside the cafeteria. This brick building, like everything else on campus, was clinical and stark. A dozen doors to large therapy rooms snaked around the corner of the hallway. My destination was fourth door on the left. To say I was intimidated to be in a group therapy session is an understatement.

The general program was a six-week stay in the hospital, on a rolling schedule, so the groups were ever changing. My group was a rotating mishmash of addicts, self-harmers, people in grief, and members of the armed forces—all of us trauma victims.

The therapy room was simple. Chairs lined three walls, each with a plastic stool under it, to prop our feet on. Wendy, the therapist, had a desk in the corner, white boards on two walls, and a bookshelf with mementos, signs, and sayings in the corner. There was also a large stack of blankets for those who got cold from the fierce air conditioning. Like old people in church, we fell into patterns of sitting in the same seats every day. I sat against the north wall, third chair from the door.

Over the course of treatment we would each share our stories. Each one carried with it a heavy burden and deep consequences.

A young army veteran was haunted by nightmares of his time served in Iraq. That, along with the loss of his mother, drove him to drown out the nightmares. He drank Wild Turkey like water. When he first arrived he was still detoxing and had tremors for weeks.

There was a sex addict who drowned out her very dysfunctional biracial, famous background with addictive behaviors. She spent years and thousands of dollars on her addiction. She would drive hours and hours for a hook-up, only to start chasing the next one.

A young mom drank wine to celebrate anything and everything, in an attempt to numb her past trauma. She told me she would open a bottle of wine and enjoy the whole thing as a reward for getting through the day with grade-school children and a toddler. She struggled with anxiety.

One of our group mates was a heroin addict. Her trauma and her relationships had drowned her. Her teenage daughters took cell phone video of her driving while she was high. She used to put heroin up her butt instead of shooting it through her veins so she could get high faster.

Another silver group member entered the room on her first day in a hooded sweatshirt and sunglasses, refusing to let anybody see her face. When we finally did see her face and arms, she was covered with cigarette burns. Self harm was her way of numbing out the expectations of her high pressure, wealthy family, and escaping from the rigor of acting in LA.

Post-Traumatic Faith

An advantage of a treatment facility can be the anonymity. Nobody knows you and without technology there is no social media or Googling to look you up. This is a comfort and allows some people, under the cloak of anonymity, to recreate themselves. For instance, Tracker told me he worked with abused women and children, sponsoring shelters, and helping with counseling. Later we found out he was there because of not only his addiction but also because he had choked his girlfriend almost to death and beat her badly. I would find out later that he was an owner of a large internet corporation and his philanthropic work may have been embellished.

One of the first tasks of therapy group was to make a timeline of your life. I took a large 11 x 17 piece of paper and sectioned it into quadrants. One column for traumatic or significant events that happened during my lifetime. Another column for memories, divided by age, 0–5, 6–10, and so on. The third column was for traumatic events that occurred in my adulthood. I had several panic attacks while working on this project. I sat in the television/living room and relived these events. The memories swirled around me and I was lost in my own history as people walked in and out of the room, either on their way to the art room or laundry rooms.

As she did every new patient, over the course of two weeks my therapist talked me through sections of my timeline, bit by bit, while everybody listened to our conversation. The power of group therapy was not lost on me. Listening to other people and how they dealt or did not deal with their trauma was informative and useful information. It felt good to not feel so alone in my pain.

At each session, which was twice a day every weekday, Wendy would check in with everybody to see how we were doing. Doctor appointments, trauma therapists, assessments, and psychiatric appointments were all held throughout the day. Usually, those appointments would disregulate and upset patients and they would need calming, reassuring, and a chance to regain perspective to shift their thinking back into the present and into being fully functional for the rest of the day.

I have counseled many people in my career as a pastor. Pastors are so often called on in the time of crisis, bereavement, and trauma. Not to minimize the need for spiritual counsel in the face of upheaval, but pastors are given such small amounts of education in mental health, in comparison to true mental health professionals, it almost seems dangerous they are the first line of defense. I could only hope to do people justice and referred to others in the mental health field when necessary. The counseling hat was the least favorite of the many hats I wore. I was bumbling in the dark, and prayed consistently that I would be wise and discerning.

Now that I have seen some extraordinary therapists, psychologists, and psychiatrists I am in awe of their work. The patience, knowledge, and wisdom it takes to unravel a lifetime of trauma is Herculean. Since returning home from the hospital eight years ago I have seen a trauma therapist consistently, twice a week. We take little pieces of information and hold them up to the light like sea glass, analyzing where the light shines through and where it is blurry or blocks out the sun. I like to think we approach my trauma like a slinky—over the years we keep coming around to the same topics, each time with better information and more useful tools to deal with it all.

Wendy, my group therapist at the hospital, was direct, no nonsense, and held a demeanor and stature that demanded respect and invited professional relationship. My first trauma therapist in Billings, Diane, was eclectic, friendly, and funny. Diane says it took two years before we could really address trauma because every time we got close to it I would dissociate and it would take the rest of the session to "get me back," which is to say reorient me to the present. Over six years we developed a working relationship that was excellent for me. She had a wonderful, dry, sarcastic humor which I loved. We made progress in identifying my trauma, some of it obvious, some of it less obvious. Her insight and careful listening helped me to trust her with secrets that nobody on the planet knew about me. Sadly, she retired.

At first I was frantic, feeling this anchoring tether in my life fraying right before my eyes. However, before I could completely fall apart she connected me with another therapist. She said, "Angela is not as funny as I am, but way smarter!" Together they overlapped my therapy allowing me to acclimate to Angela while grieving the ending of my working relationship with Diane. Trust is a hard-fought resource in my life so the six years we had working together seemed difficult to just end without lamenting its loss.

I have seen Angela for two years now and she is as wise and smart as any mental health care professional I have seen. Her insights have helped me tremendously and we continue to peek under the pieces of my fractured mind, carefully, slowly, and with hope that they become a little less scary to talk about and unravel.

Healing the mind is arduous, dry landscape but with good help it is saturated in the hope that tomorrow will be clearer and easier to breathe in than today.

27

Zoot, Emeraude, and Molly

THE MENTAL HOSPITAL WAS committed to a low stimulus environment. In addition to no caffeine or sugar, it was atmospherically quiet. It felt as if they had confused "calm" with "mute." The TV was usually not on and we were not allowed computers or phones that would provide electronic stimulus. They encouraged reading but only of the materials given to help with your treatment.

There was no music at the psych and trauma hospital, save the shitty Zen pan flute whining from a sad little sound box hiding behind ancient magazines and crusty modeling clay in the art room. However, there were a few instruments around. One patient, an airman who worked in the mental health department of the Air Force, had earned a spot at the hospital by trying to kill himself. He brought along his guitar and occasionally serenaded us with original music in the "living room." It was a wonderful disruption to the silence of the grounds. Another patient rescued a djembe from obscurity. She walked around campus, happily banging out irregular rhythms, taking pleasure in her bizarre musicality.

There was also a piano in the corner of the cafeteria. I enjoyed looking through the dusty music collection. Jazz, hymns, and popular music were tossed like mixed nuts into the random pile on top of the upright. Occasionally during breaks between lectures and therapy sessions, I would tinker my time away, alone in the cavernous room, with sunlight streaming through the large windows. I was interrupted occasionally by a patient coming through to get a drink or a piece of fruit. It was comforting to have the familiarity of music to call on during a lonely and confusing time.

Being a resident in a long-term treatment facility is a constant series of hellos and goodbyes. You share the most intimate details of your life with strangers, who become friends, then become vapors as they retreat to their lives outside our boundaries. Sometime during the last three weeks of my stay, someone took the piano music away. I'm not sure why but I was so sad. It made me feel as if I had lost yet another friend. The piano sat silent and still after that.

In Marilyn's view, all educated people played the piano. I admire the determination and sacrifice it took on her part to pay for lessons, for almost two decades, for all three of us. We were poor but somehow she managed. When I was older I was able to pay for lessons by cleaning the piano teacher's studio and taking on my own students.

Starting in 1977, I took lessons from age five until I graduated high school. I had many teachers over the years. The old lady in the little red house, the creepy man in the one room studio, and the large lady whose cloying Emeraude perfume hung in the studio like fog.

On the first year I was assigned the red John Thompson Piano Book #1. I struggled through the first few pages but then got high-centered at "Swans on the Lake" (page 11). I couldn't make heads or tails of it. Marilyn decided to help me learn. She sat down on the piano bench with a wooden spoon in her hand. Every time I made a mistake she would rap my fingers hard with the spoon. I remember crying my way through that damn song. In spite of Marilyn, I eventually mastered the song. Thus began my thirteen-year-long piano education and a nine-year battle with hating the instrument.

I wanted to be a saxophonist. People who played the sax were wild and free. I imagined myself hip and cool like the Muppets, Zoot and Janice! But I was a pianist who also wanted to be a brave, soaring vocalist. I tried. I remember singing in a trio in high school but when I went off key, my mother put her finger to her lips to shush me. I was mortified and swore off spotlight singing from then on. Yes, the neighbors said they opened their windows when I was practicing so they could hear me play piano. Yes, I had my own students when I was thirteen years old. But still. It wasn't what I wanted. I wanted to be Zoot.

Starting in high school in 1986 a beloved teacher asked me to accompany the choir on the piano. I loved everything about accompaniment. It was a place of both honor and anonymity for me. I felt like the choir enveloped me, so I was not the center of attention. I loved helping the choir find their parts during practice. There were times that I played the piano for four choirs at school, then came home and practiced another two or three hours. All the extra music I took on gave me an acceptable mental and emotional refuge at home. Music became the place I could be lost and found, all at the same time.

One teacher was particularly interesting to me. JoElla. I'm sure overprotective, ultra-religious Marilyn did not go into JoElla's house when she hired her to teach us, since the house was filled with alternative religious contraband. I poured over comic books about Hare Krishna's god, Vishnu. There were stories about Vishnu as a child and growing into a god. I consumed the Hindu traditions and prayers. JoElla allowed me to go upstairs one day and see their prayer altar. It was a small alcove on the landing of the second floor. Ornate gods and figures swam in bright colors and candlelight. Prayer icons were scattered on beautiful fabrics. Thin lines of smoke snaked through the air, bringing the smell of sandalwood and reverence to my senses. It was all mysterious and fantastical.

JoElla's husband, Steve, worked at the local grocery store in the produce department. His long wavy hair was always tied up in a net. Whenever we saw him he always greeted us cheerily. One day, while I was waiting for my brother and sister to finish their piano lessons, Steve showed me his garden in the basement. As far as I can recall, he was growing tomatoes. But it seemed so odd to me that he was growing so many tomatoes under black lights in his basement and especially in the closet. Can you even smoke tomatoes?

After some time at home following my hospital stay in 2015, I was so keen on getting off all the medications that I thought I would try another way. The medical doctor who christens those worthy of a medical marijuana card works in a run-down, dark, shingled building on Grand Avenue in Billings, Montana. Walking into the office is like a step back in time to what I imagine a seventies doctor's office would look like. Dark wood floor, narrow windows with little light shining through their unwashed panes. A pleasantly round secretary greeted me at the open door of a very cluttered office with her little dog yipping around her skirt. With her cigarette-laden breath she offered forms to fill out on a clipboard and pointed me to the waiting room. The mismatched orange, green, and brown chairs welcomed me to the otherwise colorless room. Peeking out of the top of the jute hanging plant holders was little bit of green plant.

And then, color burst into the room. The doctor came out of his converted bedroom office in a purple shiny suit. He wore a yellow shirt and orange shoes. His hair was a mussy blond piled up like Billy Idol. He greeted me enthusiastically and ushered me into the office. We sat. I looked at him and thought, "If you are trying to convince me that medical marijuana does not mess up your brain, based on the colorful and zany looks of you, it's not working." "You have complex-PTSD?" he asked, even though he had my papers right in front of him. "You *are* on a lot of medications," he said. "We can get you off of *all* of those," he promised. I was simultaneously optimistic and pessimistic. Within five minutes I had my form signed for a medical marijuana card. Five minutes to diagnose and prescribe a panacea for my ills.

I would need to connect with a provider, so I chose a business card from the dozen offerings that were on a long, glass table in the waiting room. I made my choice solely on the neat and tidy design of the business card.

I gave marijuana a *really* good try. I tried vaping, smoking, and edibles. The edible gummy bears and mini muffins hit hard and fast. I would get so high I would sit and watch the clouds in the sky swim in their blue ocean for hours. Because I had a teenage daughter still at home, I felt as if I couldn't be high all the time, and I hated the feeling anyway. I liked vaping most because I could avoid the THC and only vape the CBD. By the time I quit my trial, I was vaping the strength that you give cancer patients at the end of life to camouflage their pain. And I felt nothing. Nothing at all. I wasn't high, and I wasn't cured. I was, however, more depressed that nothing was working. Dr. Billy Idol be damned. His promises were as dried up as the weed I smoked.

28

God of My Understanding

For as long as I can remember, Jesus was real to me—a visceral, formidable presence in my daily life. I met him at an age younger than I can remember. Being raised in the church gave me ample opportunity to absorb the ethos of what good can come from being part of a community of faith. Childhood innocence protected me from growing to hate the institution and its people who would fail to protect me.

In the summer of 1987, on the gorgeous Orcas Island in the San Juan archipelago, off the coast of Washington state, I made a commitment that would direct the trajectory of my life for three decades. On August 24, I separated myself from the main group and wandered the warm wooded area by myself. As I felt the forest absorb the sound of my feet on the dirt path, the rustle of the leaves and foliage and the talking of the birds, I prayed. Prayer, as much about the silence of listening as it is about talking, was a comfort to me. I sought peace. I craved love.

As I walked through the woods I felt an inaudible but deeply impressionable feeling of being called, invited, and compelled to become a minister. More specifically, I knew I wanted to spend my life serving God in the church. Something about the potential of the church, when on its best behavior, beckoned me. The church did not earn my trust. I was just a heart that chose to believe it could be good and pledged my life to that end.

And then I did get to serve God in the church. I spent twenty-five years invested in nurturing the faith of myself, my family, and others. I have been privileged to be a youth pastor, children's pastor, education pastor, co-lead pastor, and have been a part of starting three churches.

But after my breakdown I felt like I joined the ranks of singles, introverts, the queer community, artists, doubters, divorcees, addicts, non-English speakers, graveyard shifters, one-parent families, individuals with developmental or intellectual disabilities, and liberals, all misfits within mainstream evangelical church culture. I felt like I was a sock without a match because of my mental illness.

When I returned from the hospital my anxiety automatically made church a big pile of no. My stomach would sour at the thought of being around so many people, having to hug/touch them, and deal with the noise. Even the thought was exhausting and made me sick to my stomach. My anti-anxiety meds and earplugs weren't enough to keep me from shaking profusely, sweating, and having a crazy heartbeat.

This place I have loved for the entirety of my life had become an edifice of challenges that reinforced the feeling that I no longer fit in, when I had been one of its greatest proponents. People would encourage me to "work myself back in" as if just going for a few minutes more each week would inoculate me to the symptoms of my mental illness.

At the hospital, every night, every patient was required to go to a 12-step meeting. The offerings were Narcotics Anonymous (NA), Alcoholics Anonymous (AA), Sex and Love Addicts (SLA), Sex and Love Addicts for men (SLAM), and Co-dependents Anonymous (CODA). Sometimes I went to the NA meetings, because they were better run than the others. I went to at least three meetings a week, a valiant effort on my part, that fell dismally short of the seven required. My addiction, being a workaholic, did not fall into a category for a small group, so a friend and I used to skip the meetings, hiding in the art room or our rooms, avoiding the nurses. If they found us they would say, "You know we have to write you up if you don't go to a meeting." "Yes," we would say. They would ask, "Why are you skipping meetings?" It seemed inappropriate to say, "Because they are so frustrating they may drive me to drink." They would write us up but nothing ever came of it. What were they going to do? Kick us out?

One of the challenges I had with the AA programs was Step #2 "We came to believe that a power greater than ourselves could restore us to sanity." So much of the discussion in meetings is gathered around one's higher power. When Bill Wilson wrote the big book for the AA program he stated that he could only connect to a higher power "if not related to spiritual belief and religion."

In meetings I heard everything from, "My kids are my higher power," "My (dead) dogs are my higher power," and, I kid you not, "My fish are my higher power." How in the ever-loving-earth are our kids our higher power? How are they a power greater than ourselves that restore us to sanity? My kids are amazing but they aren't our higher power. They about drove us insane some days. And dogs, fish, horses, etc. How are they a power greater than ourselves? What was Bill looking for? I realize that AA has helped thousands and thousands of people. I don't deny the power and significance of the program he authored. I just get high-centered on that one point.

I've only ever known a spiritual higher power and I don't know how else to define it if not through deity. Jesus Christ—God the Son, God the Father, God the Holy Spirit—three in one, the trinity, my higher power. I cannot divorce the concept of higher power from God. My God, the one in whom I choose to place my trust, the God of my understanding, is a creative creator, a loving divinity, a just judge in a fallen world, a wise friend and trusted companion. My God does not answer to me but does answer me, although not always in the way I want.

I believe in the God in the way I understand the Jesuit Catholics do. We believe that God walks with us through the valleys of our life and over the hilltops. He is not a sadistic dictator or disengaged spectator from the sidelines. To me, the personhood of God has a sense of "withness" that is both personal and complete.

Some may say, "Well, isn't your life an example of God not answering prayers?" I don't know how to respond to that. Yes, I prayed consistently that God would free me from the abuse of others. But, somewhere, preserved deep inside me, there is a vein of grace that runs deep and pulses with love. Through that love we have raised four children, pastored many churches, and loved many people. Not perfectly, but with good intentions. So, is that an example of goodness preserved in me by my own doing or did something higher, greater than myself give me the gifts to overcome and survive my circumstances? I am confident that I could not do that for myself. My higher power stepped in and did that for me.

I have heard it said that what you are thinking about the most in any given moment is your higher power. There is some truth to that. If I think about monetary success every minute of the day, that can become a navigating and driving force, a higher power. Career, pets, hobbies, obsessions, all can usurp divinity in the place of a higher power, if we give it that kind of focus.

So, do I have a higher power? Yes. It is Jesus Christ, whom I believe to be omniscient, omnipresent, and omnipotent. I believe in the message of love he stood for, lived, and promoted, and I choose to further what I believe his message of love and grace was and is.

29

Grave Robbing

Marilyn was a grave robber. She loved old cemeteries. Any time she saw one she would veer off the road and we would wander among the headstones. We read the births and deaths of people and wondered about the lives represented by the dash in between those dates. However, if she saw something interesting on an old grave, she would take it. For years a very large coffee pot, similar to the ones that would be used over a campfire, graced our mantle. She pulled that off a grave. We also had two crockery pots and different old tin cans that people had put on graves to put flowers in. Those too joined our house decor, filled with dried flowers and baby's breath.

    I don't know where Marilyn is buried. I didn't go to her funeral. From 1990 to her death in 2021, she insisted she would not see or talk to me unless I told everybody who knew about the child abuse "allegations" that I had lied. She wanted me to clear her name. When Dana' was sick from her addiction Marilyn got in touch with her and reconciled—to the point that Dana' moved from Texas, put her stuff in storage in Missouri and moved in with Marilyn. For two weeks. Marilyn also got in touch with Park when he was deathly sick from heart complications due to diabetes. But she never forgave me. She sent my letters back unopened and hung up on my phone calls. It was clear she was done with me. Eventually, the fog of dementia and cancer left her with no connection to the outside world. I felt I was honoring her wishes by not attending her memorial. I didn't need the closure. I had been processing that for thirty-one years.

Grave Robbing

I don't remember the day or year Jay died. It didn't matter much to me. He was a father in name but he violated the trust and innocence of two helpless little girls in the most egregious way, by raping them and then disappearing for the majority of their lives. Jay cut off all relationship with us once we brought to light all that he had done. Many years later my brother begged me to go to Jay's funeral with him. I explained that I didn't see Jay as a father—he was just a man who hurt me. While Park, who was eleven years old when they divorced, remembered Jay as a dad, I have absolutely no memory of his presence in the house in Reno. The halls echoed with the sounds of women and children but never the bass of a man's voice. I don't remember eating meals together at the oddly green varnished dining room table with its big fat elephant-like legs. There are no memories of lying together on the scratchy orange den carpet listening to my favorite records. The long gravel driveway extending from the dark brown garage doors to the street didn't have impressions of his big feet walking near my little ones.

Death is strange. I sat once with a family whose wife/daughter/mother had died. The young woman had thrown a lung embolism. Blood was everywhere. The heroic nurses manually bagged her for two hours to keep her alive, even though she was technically already dead. They did this so the Native American family would be able to say goodbye to her spirit. It was an odd conundrum. The family wanted to light sage and do a smudging to cleanse her energy and say goodbye. However, she was being given oxygen to keep her "alive," and in a hospital, so clearly lighting anything was not an option. The desperate family placed the newborn baby next to her, hoping the mama would rally when she felt her baby next to her skin.

It was a chaotic room, filled with two loud, opinionated, and feuding families. The Caucasian husband and family wanted nothing to do with the smudging and soul preservation. He just wanted his wife back. Her Indian family was desperate to honor her properly, traditionally. At one point I kicked a combative family member out of the room. I told her not to come back until she could control her emotions and words. "You are bringing far too much drama and chaos to an already emotionally charged situation," I said. She went to the car, came back with a Gatorade bottle filled with alcohol. She became much tamer after she drank that. The hospital room was in such turmoil, with weeping and arguing, that when it came time to do the death pronouncement, the doctor instructed me to tell the room instead of doing it himself. And then I listened as the husband lay next to his deceased wife, embracing her one last time while wailing. The six-day old infant still lay by her mother's now cold leg. One of the most humbling things a minister can do is walk a family through the death of a loved one. The experience is beautiful, tragic, and bonding. Those moments were precious but life changing.

I once had an opportunity to photograph a baby who had no chance of survival. She was born beautiful. Perfect little lips. Eight perfect toes. Little fingers she kept trying to fit into her mouth. I photographed her with her parents loving tenderly on her. I took pictures of them crouched around the bassinet where she lay dying, because the nurses said holding her would overstimulate the body and hasten her death. She died half a day after she was born. To pray strength, blessing, and unexpected peace over them was an unmatched honor. I stood outside the room as the baby slipped from life and then listened to the desperate cries of the parents after losing their child. It was heartrending.

There is something healing in tears. They express our emotions but more importantly, they cleanse the soul. It is a soul "reset." But my emotional meter is broken. That little girl who stared herself down in the mirror, forcing herself to not feel anything and not to cry, is still present. She is still scared the wrong emotion matched with the wrong person or timing will warrant catastrophe. Truth be told, sometimes I fake emotion just to feel as if I fit into a situation but sometimes, to my horror, it comes bursting out of me, uninvited. In an unguarded moment fear, anger, sadness, or loneliness can erupt on the scene, causing me to emotionally scramble for cover because I am sure something bad is going to happen. However, I want to have full-fledged, grown up, developed emotions but that seems a far cry from the stoney silence I generally sit in.

30

Window Shopping

Even though I love fall, my mood begins to sink when the season arrives. No amount of falling leaves, pumpkin spice, or apple pie candles can lift it. I feel a black fog of depression taking over and it doesn't move until late January. It's a rhythm I have come to expect from life but one I will continue to fight.

My birthday is in late October. The worst birthday I have experienced was when I was in the hospital. I had been a resident there for six weeks and there was no sign they were going to let me out any time soon. The depression, confusion, and loneliness made the day fall flat.

Every fall and winter season I need support. Being in my fifties I understand the need for support more than ever. Support stockings and spandex foundation garments occupy a decent amount of space in my dresser. And the girls. They need support too. For all the fashion faux pas that it is, I really would prefer the comfort of a sports bra every day. But sports bras could make a sub sandwich into a panini. I need more support than that. Support is crucial.

But growing up I didn't get the support I needed during the holiday season. I got falsified holidays and Hallmark channel movie reenactments.

In the late 1970s, when we lived on Roosevelt Street in Coeur d'Alene, I remember always having a Christmas dinner party. Marilyn would put on her long, plaid, old-fashioned dress, with a white apron. She invited people who had no place to go. We pushed the big table up against the bay window and covered it with a starched white tablecloth in preparation for the food everybody would bring. Marilyn, completely transformed, was sweet, engaging and fun. We created an artificial Norman Rockwell family for the day. The extra people in the house were an insulation against her anger.

Every year on Marilyn's birthday, December 9, our little family put up the Christmas tree. The tree was never artificial. She would only have a real tree. We would decorate it with old fashioned ornaments, some of which I still have, and handmade ones from school. Looking at our tree was like following a trail of memories. It was a timeline of our childhood.

My sixth grade year, I received a green wicker plastic sewing basket for Christmas. It had a few sewing accoutrements and I loved it. My other present was a pair of Levis and a button-down blue dress shirt. This was what cool sixth graders wore and I wanted to look like the other kids. Keeping in mind that the dress code rules for public schools, according to Marilyn, was three dresses a week, dress pants once a week, and jeans once a week. I was never going to look like all the other kids but I wanted to try.

The Christmas jeans were too big for my slender body. Marilyn gathered them at the waist, sewing them so they would fit. This created little puckers along the fabric but I was so proud to wear them. However, on the first day I wore them, one of my fellow sixth graders in Mr. Couser's class said, "You look like you have a penis," referencing one of the puckers. I was crushed and never wore them again.

There weren't always Christmas gifts. One year there was nothing under the tree. My high school crush and I picked up a box the church had given us. That night we waded through the falling, sparkling snow in the yard to deliver it to my house. The church had provided us with a box of food and some small gifts for us kids. I received a pair of rather ugly crocheted slippers that were slippery and deadly on the basement stairs and on the kitchen linoleum.

The day after Christmas my ninth grade year, Marilyn left Sandy. He was visiting his kids in Texas. She moved us into an old house on Fourth Street that eventually became a law office. Dead of winter in North Idaho and the house had no heat. We holed up in the kitchen with one small space heater, slept bundled up in frigid bedrooms, and hoarded the space heater when we had to shower.

Christmas 1989 was an ugly one. I remember the air was heavy with unspoken words and anxiety, but I don't recall why. Dana' and Park were home for a bit, having reconciled, at least on the surface, with Marilyn. Dana' was living in California and Park was working on cruise ships, playing piano for the guests in the restaurants and lounges. Despite the holiday, the mood was increasingly ominous.

After they left, Marilyn quit talking to me. The silence smothered me in a thick blanket of dread. Within days the dam broke. I don't recall the precipitating event. I just remember the rage.

Marilyn picked me up and threw me across the room. Not only was I conditioned to not fight back but also there was no way I could match her strength. Then she picked me up again and threw me against the wall in my small bedroom, which was only big enough for a twin bed. I bounced off the wall onto the bed. I clearly remember her throwing a handful of pencils and pens into the room at me. One of the pencils ricocheted off the wall and stuck in the low Styrofoam ceiling like an arrow.

That was really the last time Marilyn ever spoke to me. She imposed the silent treatment after that and resorted to putting nasty notes in my lunch box about my behavior or how badly she disliked me. Every day I cried on the bus on the way to school, desperate to escape my life. The silence continued into February.

Every day when I came home from school. I called Marilyn at work, as required, to tell her I was home. She would answer the phone in her pleasant work voice and then hang up without responding as soon as she heard my voice. Then, I sat on the couch in the dark house and cried until 4:30 at which time I got up. I turned the lights on and sat at the piano, playing bright, happy music for her to come home to. It was dangerous for me to show I was unhappy, so I hid it in the music.

Christmas carries with it such conflicting emotions. Memories of years past overwhelm the current holiday. For years I created wonderful Christmas celebrations for congregations and communities. I felt the pressure to celebrate even though I suspected most people's celebrations were stuffed with superficial joy. My own attempts at celebrating seemed flat. I felt as if I was creating wonderful holiday window displays for people to enjoy but I could never quite get on the other side of the glass, on the sidewalk where the real party and joy was.

Holidays now are raucous and fun. On a lucky year, all four children and their families are home to celebrate with us. Our little house bulges at the seams to hold all the loved ones. Babies, toddlers, young adults, and us old folks, all jockeying to get a word in edgewise. There's nothing I like more than when all "my" people are under my roof. And yet, sometimes I am still trapped on the inside of the window, while they get to play on the outside.

31

Surviving Childhood

AT THE HOSPITAL, I had a large gorgeous scenic photograph on a canvas that a friend had sent me. The picture was such a lovely gift because there were no decorations on the walls of the rooms. I had been allowed exactly one thumbtack to hang it on the wall. Really, I was in more danger from the canvas falling off the wall than I was from the thumbtack! But, I packaged up the photograph along with the contents of my little dorm room of almost twelve weeks, mailing boxes home of clothing and books.

There was no fanfare, no send off, no friends waving goodbye. I left early in the morning just as I had arrived, in obscurity and alone.

I caught an early morning van off the little compound that had become my home. Navigating through the airports, with the cacophony of noise and chaos was a challenge, even with earplugs. Upon returning home one of the most common questions people asked was, "Do you feel better?" Well, no. I had only just begun to explore the tip of the iceberg that was my mental health. The clinicians had done a good job at educating me on what challenges I was facing but I lacked applied understanding. I would not be able to define that until I was living in a "real world" environment. I just told people that now I had better questions.

The real world was a shock to my system. The combination of medication, toxic shame over my mental health diagnosis, overstimulation, and sheer emotional exhaustion left my confidence shattered and emotions raw.

Surviving Childhood

When I entered the hospital I had a job, relationships, and goals. When I came home I could not go back to work. All my projects and speaking engagements had been guillotined by my absence and unsure future. My bosses directed me to focus exclusively on my health. Friends and family did an awkward dance around me trying to figure out what I needed and wanted. I became convinced I had become an agoraphobic. I would break into cold sweats and shake if I was in a store or group setting of any kind. Oddly enough, especially Walmart. But anybody who doesn't quake in Walmart has a special kind of Zen that I don't possess.

I was on too many medications to be safely driving, which didn't matter because I didn't have a desire to see anybody or go anywhere. For months I did not do laundry, cook, clean, or do anything more than sitting on the couch. I went to yoga five hours a week, a therapist twice a week, and squeezed in the frequent visits with a psychiatrist. This was the totality of my life. I was a raw wound with no scab to hide beneath while I heal.

After eight years of this the only thing I am 100 percent certain of is that this season is an exercise of surrender and trust. I have doctors, therapists, pastors, and spiritual directors who help chart my path forward. I hear the voice of God through them as they synchronistically yet independently speak words of caution, wisdom, and patience. What an amazing gift my "village" is to me.

I have never understood the concept of being a work in process more than I do now. I am incomplete and I know it.

Ideally, childhood should be savored, not "survived." Survival is for prisoners of war, people who triumph over cancer, and Black Friday shoppers. But I survived my childhood. I survived an orphanage, adoptions, and physical, emotional, and sexual abuse. The most horrific memories are still buried deep, surfacing only in my nightmares.

There is something heady, a pride and strength, in being a survivor. We like the idea of the warrior who fights against the odds to conquer the foe. However, being a survivor isn't what makes me strong or confident. It is the ability to point to my wounds that stand witness to my pain and say "it still hurts" or "I need help" that puts me square in the lap of love and grace. But I wonder. Is surviving enough? Or is there more?

Looking back at my life as a landfill that needs sorting and excavation seems to fly in the face of my "look for the sunrise" philosophy. But I am kept hopeful and alive by the fact that I can see how far I have come.

Post-Traumatic Faith

When my emotional tsunami rose unexpectedly, it flipped everything on its head. Instead of carrying pride at being a survivor, riding the waves with confidence, I was forced to admit that I was a victim. Instead of preaching about overcoming, I had to acknowledge that some events of my life held pieces of my soul captive. My optimistic focus of being one who rose above was buried by the reality of one who was just trying to survive the flashbacks, nightmares, anxiety, and depression.

Something about the experience of needing to be taken care of for so many months, not being able to care for my children, of living in solitude, losing career, relationships, and independence has dampened my confidence. I still act confident, but even I don't believe myself.

My brain may never recover from that breakdown. My memory hasn't returned to full capacity and my concentration remains stilted. I have struggled to write this book, sometimes writing a complete chapter, forgetting about it and rewriting it all over again, only to find it later. As I write, I go back through my notes over and over to remember what I have said in the past chapters. Throughout my days, I have to pause to remember details that should be easy to recall. I exhaust easily and cannot handle groups of people or frantic activity or noise for very long.

I used to find value in being known and receiving atta-girls from my work. My other-esteem craves someone to call me out and pat me on the back for something, anything. I feel as if I have disappeared from the sight of the living, breathing, thriving world.

I still check my email five times a day as if I am going to miss something really urgent. I look at social media twice that often. Mostly I do it so I have something to do. I leave unanswered voicemails on my phone just so there is a number that pops up instead of "nobody called you."

I want to work more. Do more. I am anxious to get "back in the game." Every invitation and job opportunity that wafts past me piques my interest and I want to say "*Yes*! Pick me! I want to do that!" I miss the busyness and interactions. And then days like today happen. After a couple of very busy days, I am barely functioning. I'm tired, overwhelmed, and want to stay in bed all day.

"Overwhelmed" can be a code word for anxiety or depression. For me, it means my mind has difficulty prioritizing life. My brain is equally overwhelmed by the bathroom needing more toilet paper as it is by my daughter's wedding that is happening next month. To the overwhelmed brain, all details hang heavy in the balance, no matter their size.

The doctors have told me very clearly that I am not ready to work full time. I need more time to rest and figure out how to recognize and answer my own needs. They have warned me of the devastating effects another mental collapse would have and I listen.

Life has become less about producing and more about clawing my way to the surface for air. I loved being a pastor. I would still be doing it, to my detriment, if life hadn't intervened. I feel useless and lost without the interactions, relationships, and community that my work provided. I never really thought I put that much weight in my job or took that much identity from it. I didn't think I wore it as a badge of distinction. Until it was gone. Then I felt a little like a societal deadweight.

I fell asleep the other night crying. The last thing I remember sobbing about was "but I don't want to be a writer!" It isn't that I don't love writing or appreciate the impact well-placed words can have on lives. It is just that I imagined my life to be totally different right now. I'm a teacher, pastor, preacher, leader. I'm supposed to be at the microphone, not sequestered to my desk writing in anonymity. If this sounds like a temper tantrum, it is. If it sounds like ingratitude, it is. I'm working through it.

Now, I write. I paint, I'm a mommy, wife, grammy, and art enthusiast who loves her doggie. I am a composite of the things I love and the things I dreamed. I'm Jill with C-PTSD, depression, anxiety, weight obsession, and a dissociative disorder. But here's the thing. Not one of those things is the definition of me, my soul, or my worth. (I say this with more conviction than I feel.)

As the new year looms, it is a blank slate of possibility. Last year has been colored on, spilled on, shrunk in the dryer and spoiled. Luckily the new year is a fresh box of crayons, and it's mine for the taking.

I love calendars and journal books. They thrill me down to my calloused toes. I also find them paralyzing. At some point I have to commit, mark my territory. I write my name. But something in me is never happy with how that first mark looks; but I have to live with it nonetheless. It's mine. I have claimed it. Let the messing up of it begin.

That same kind of "I don't want to ruin it" angst looms in these first hours of the new year. I want this year to be better than the last. So I create unrealistic rules and guidelines so that the year will remain unspoiled. These rules are new car promises. We swear we won't eat in the new car, spill coffee, or let so much as a bug fart, in order to preserve the new smell and dignity of the purchase. Six months down the road we are kicking French fries under the seat so they won't get ground into the floor mats. We know it is going to happen but we can't help ourselves from making promises.

So this year I'm going to lose sixty pounds by never cheating on my diet, read my Bible every day, and talk to Jesus nicely. I will never look at Facebook on my phone while on the toilet. I'm going to work out every single day and drink my body weight in water to make sure that I am properly hydrated. I will plan ahead, not procrastinate, and meet every single deadline. I will not fight with my husband or frustrate my children, and the sun is going to shine out of my ass 365 days this year.

Clearly, I need realistic goals and dreams. I just don't know how to set my intentions honestly without perjuring myself in the process. I wish I could find one person who meets their new year's resolutions, so I could learn from them. Maybe they could teach me how to create a big enough bucket to hold my expectations but small enough to not overwhelm. In the meantime, I'm still going to take my shot at accomplishing world peace and winning the Mrs. America crown.

Sometimes reality and my perception are out of sync with one another. I write for two magazines, and I write a blog that has been viewed thousands of times. I have a podcast that people have been listening to all over the world. The responses to my work are warm, encouraging, and reinforcing of my love of the written word and affirming of my talent. And yet, I still feel like a hangnail.

Where is the line between celebrating value and over-valuing what one does?

In the silence I discovered a truth. I needed me. I desperately needed to care for my body, mind, and spirit. Every day now life begins with "what do I need today to take care of myself?" and I try to do only those things. I take care of myself. Wise leaders tell me, "Your vocation is self-care." I exercise hard in a gym five days a week. I write, draw, knit, and paint. I make sure I go to my doctor appointments and take medications four times a day. I sit on the couch with the kids and watch TV shows. I read books. And I'm alive. I'm no longer speedwalking through life but really living.

Eight years ago, not a day went by that I didn't crave being needed by others because I thought that meant I belonged somewhere, to someone. I am learning that people will take as much from you as you are willing to give. We are all some version of junior high students engrossed only in ourselves, largely oblivious to those around us. To live well, be well, we must protect ourselves, mind, body, and spirit. We cannot delegate that task to anybody else.

I would like to say that I'm all better. I'm healed. I'm back better than ever. But depression, anxiety, and flashbacks still roll in but now so do joy, peace, and thankfulness. It's a mixed bag of balancing the past with the present, not allowing the past memories to hijack the beauty of the present moments I have been given.

I have given birth four times, overcome unimaginable abuse, sat successfully for comprehensive exams, been a pastor for over two decades, survived celebrating New Year's Eve with the Mexicans, and overcome OCD control of my sock drawer. Now I can enjoy being myself and breathe in the beautiful moments that used to escape my grasp.

I feel the stilling of the Jell-O that has been my confidence. I can feel it quickening like slow-cured cement into something strong, like a bone graft that becomes stronger than the original bone. To succumb to the weight of a tragic childhood, diseases that have affected friends and family, the loss of loved ones, the suicides and unexpected tragedies I have witnessed, would be a tragedy. To deny their impact on my life would be an even larger one because that would be to refuse the grace of survival that I have been gifted.

I am so grateful for the time that I was able to be inpatient in a treatment facility, not just to identify my illnesses but also to help me focus on what needs to happen to keep me healthy in the future. I was given the gift of time to reflect on my life but every one of us has the opportunity to do that. Perhaps we lack the motivation to reflect because we don't understand the gifts on the other side of reflection, a deeper understanding of self, renewed focus on what is important, better physical health, improved mental and emotional health. It's worth the quest.

I have been asked many times how I can forgive those who wounded me, stole my innocence, and wielded the Bible as an excuse to abuse me.

There was a time when I had to say to myself, almost every minute "I forgive." It was a blanket statement covering all who I felt offended or hurt me. But by saying it over and over on repeat it slowly became less of a mantra and more of a lifestyle. Forgiveness isn't solely about a moment. It is truly an attitude that stands witness to the fact that even the most egregious of faults can be overcome by a grace that doesn't come from ourselves but from our faith.

At some point I didn't have to remind myself every minute that there needed to be forgiveness for me to walk forward. It became every five minutes, than every half hour until only in the moments when I hurt the worst and wanted someone to blame did I need to recall and breathe the words "I forgive."

At the end of the day isn't that what we all want? To be recognized that we are people who make mistakes. There is accountability, reconciliation, restitution, and consequences for our actions. But to those who harm others we must also consider that grace was offered freely to us and others deserve that also.

Forgiveness has not wiped away the memory of what was lost, stolen, or what hurt was caused. It does however free me from repeating a pattern of hurt and hatred that was offered to me. On good days I offer grace. On bad days I repeat to myself "I forgive"—hoping others will offer the same to me.

I have learned to find peace in the stillness because I know God is there. There is no distraction of myself and my own feeble attempts to win the grace of One who gives it freely. It is in the blackness, the quiet, and the silence that I am secure because it is where I feel the most securely held.

I have had four back surgeries, a hysterectomy, tubal ligation, gall bladder removed, both shoulders operated on, and more bladder surgeries than I can count. This means that, not only am I one of our medical systems favorite patients, but also that my body is marked with scars. Not just scars, keloids—thick raised scars.

My scars, while ugly, show triumph over previous wounds. The wounds have healed over and left an indelible mark on my skin. In my opinion, this tapestry of scars weaves a beautiful story of what my body has been through.

I am three weeks out from my fourth back surgery. The incisions are healing but are partially still scabbed over. The scabs itch and hurt. I want to scratch them off so the healing will go faster. But they go at their own pace and I have come to realize scabs are nothing more than future scars. A scab is an unhealed, yet healing wound. A scar is the triumph, the successful healing.

My heart, mind, and emotions have both scabs and scars, not the least of which is one called shame. I was afraid no one would believe me if I told them what our home was really like. I was ashamed of who I was and of what they had done to me. Our family looked amazing from the exterior, a beautiful mirage of good manners and accomplishments. Unfortunately, the interior of our lives resembled an episode of *Hoarders*—deep secrets, carried guilt, and garbage saved up from past generations. Useless, dangerous clutter.

The irony is, I learned how to keep the truth secret from even myself, so I remained an open wound. My dissociative disorder protected me by blocking so many painful memories. Now, together with my therapist, psychiatrist, pastors, education, and so many supportive friends and family I am finally able to begin to let the wounds scab over and heal.

It isn't easy acknowledging the scorched, barren emotional landscape of my past. However, I am learning those secrets aren't mine to own and I am letting them out, one by one. It's time to let others carry their own shame and responsibility. Their power shatters in the light.

I have so much gratitude for those who have helped me along the way. To all those healers in my life, I am deeply grateful for your skill and determination to help me see light in the darkest of days. For the multiple families that God has brought into my life and more friends and love than I even know, I am grateful. I am deeply humbled by the many churches and organizations that have patiently let me lead and learn. My husband and our children are evidence of the goodness of God and the bedrock of my life.

May my scars be representative of the healing that God has brought and a triumph over circumstances and people that sought to drown me. May those scars be gathered together, like music notes on a page, and create a beautiful song of grace for all to hear.

Afterword

Dear friend,

This has been a challenging journey to share with you. It has not been smooth and fluid, like syrup flowing out of a jug. Rather it feels like somebody left the lid off the peanut butter jar and I have to dig the dry bits out, one chunk at a time! However, the mining process was so good for me. I did not do this alone. The assistance of therapists, doctors, friends, and family has been essential.

My critique of the church is just one person's experience. I know there are so many who have been wounded by the institution of the church. I am sorry. I hope you are able to find not a perfect community of faith, but one that is self aware, able to correct their direction when needed, and who love with the abandon of a child with a new Christmas puppy. There is no perfect church because it is a Popsicle stick house. Every support is crucial but it's the glue that is the star. Our faith is the glue. Not our faith in one another or in the god who is misrepresented as a dictator or permissive parent, rather the Jesus of the Bible who loves deeply, perfectly. I did not have my faith banked in the churches who failed to protect me. It was not invested in the people, who so often get the love thing wrong. Rather it is deposited, backed by my full faith in my Savior Jesus Christ.

Thank you for reading. Continue on your quest toward mental, emotional, and spiritual health. It's worth the excavation.

www.ingramcontent.com/pod-product-compliance
Lightning Source LLC
Chambersburg PA
CBHW031500160426
43195CB00010BB/1039